world's
CRAZIEST
football matches

First published in 2014 by New Holland Publishers Pty Ltd
London • Sydney • Auckland

The Chandlery Unit 114 50 Westminster Bridge Road London SE1 7QY United Kingdom
1/66 Gibbes Street Chatswood NSW 2067 Australia
218 Lake Road Northcote Auckland New Zealand

www.newhollandpublishers.com

A record of this book is held at the British Library and the National Library of Australia.

ISBN 9781742575704

Managing Director: Fiona Schultz
Publisher: Alan Whiticker
Project Editor: Emily Carryer
Designer: Andrew Quinlan
Photographs: Shutterstock
Production Director: Olga Dementiev
Printer: Toppan Leefung Printing Ltd (China)

10 9 8 7 6 5 4 3 2 1

Keep up with New Holland Publishers on Facebook
www.facebook.com/NewHollandPublishers

world's
CRAZIEST
football matches

Colin Mitchell

NEW
HOLLAND

CONTENTS

Chapter 1: Amazing Games   *Page 11*

1: Liverpool 3 AC Milan 3

2: Newcastle United 4 Arsenal 4

3: Portsmouth 8 Reading 4

4: Italy 1 France 1

5: Tottenham Hotspur 3 Manchester United 5

6: Liverpool 4 Arsenal 4

7: Manchester United 8 Arsenal 2

8: Manchester United 1 Manchester City 6

10: Charlton Athletic 8 Huddersfield Town 6

10: Bayern Munich 1 Chelsea 1

11: Nottingham Forest 1 Manchester United 8

12: Manchester United 2 Bayern Munich 1

13: Liverpool 4 Newcastle United 3

14: West Bromwich Albion 2 Woking 4

15: Real Madrid 8 Eintracht Frankfurt 3

16: Wimbledon 1 Liverpool 0

17: Newcastle United 5 Manchester United 0

18: Bristol City 0 Hull City 1

19: Arsenal 4 Tottenham Hotspur 4

20: Inter Milan 0 AC Milan 6

21: Manchester United 1 Chelsea 1

22: Blackpool 4 Bolton Wanderers 3

23: England 4 West Germany 2

24: Manchester United 4 Manchester City 3

25: Manchester City 3 Queens Park Rangers 2

26: Bolton Wanderers 2 West Ham United 0

27: Barcelona v Real Madrid, El Clasico

28: Rangers v Celtic, Old Firm derby

29: Manchester United 9 Ipswich Town 0

30: Brazil 4 Italy 1

31: Germany 1 England 5

32: England 3 Hungary 6

33: Newcastle United 8 Sheffield Wedneday 0

34: Tottenham Hotspur 9 Wigan Athletic 1

35: Bournemouth 11 Margate 0

36: Celtic 2 Inter Milan 1

37: Liverpool 5 Alavés 4

38: West Germany 3 Hungary 2

39: France 2 Portugal 1

40: Portugal 0 Greece 1

41 Brazil 1 Germany 7

Did You Know?

Chapter 2: Bad Boys   *Page 102*

2.1 The Bad Boys of Football

2.2 Numbers Game

2.3 Footballers Days Off?

Did You Know?

Chapter 3. Fight Club!   *Page 118*

Fight Club: When Players Scrap

Paying the Price

Stars Who Rock…Musical Players!

Did You Hear?

Chapter 4: Secrets of the Stars   *Page 135*

Top Trivia

Chapter 5: The Crazy World of…   *Page 146*

Postponed

Roman Pavlyuchenko

Marcus Hahnemann: Hard-Rocking Keeper

Stephen Ireland: His Strange World

Zlatan Ibrahimovic: Flawed Genius

Mario Balotelli: Fireworks and Madness

Paolo Di Canio: the Loveable Eccentric

Did You Hear?

Chapter 6: The Referees   *Page 165*

Ref Justice: Shocking Decisions

Oi, Referee! Amazing Incidents

Superstitions

Biters and Spitters

Did You Know?

Chapter 7: The World According to…   *Page 178*

Gordon Strachan

Ian Holloway

Harry Redknapp

José Mourinho

Mick McCarthy

Top Trivia

Chapter 8: Strange But True   *Page 193*

Bet That Hurt! Weird Injuries

Fantastic Fans: The Super Supporters

Ball Boys Who Influenced Games!

Top Trivia

Chapter 9: Game Changers   *Page 208*

Wild Incidents From Top Fixtures

And the Keeper Scores!

Mighty Mistakes: Matches That Ended With The Wrong Score!

Mental Mascots – Furry, Funny and Crackers

Kit Clangers – When The Shirts Didn't Fit!

Animal Antics: Beasts That Have Interrupted Games

Top Trivia

Chapter 10: Memorable Moments, Biggest Wins and   *Page 231*

Other Important Lists

INTRODUCTION

We watch football, celebrate the highs and goals and sulk following crushing defeats and terrible performances. Cracking goals stick in our memories. Horrific injuries are etched on our brains forever. Some fans can remember the scores in vital games. Those fans with even better memories even remember the times of goals and who created the chances. But most football supporters remember not just the big games involving their own club and international teams, they can also talk about game-changing moments in massive fixtures around the world.

Many fans remember details that didn't even affect the outcome of a match—the antics of mascots, useless trivia, terrace chants and other football minutiae that can be the talk of school playgrounds, pubs and clubs.

Football makes us laugh, cry, celebrate and commiserate. Games, results, scorers, good and bad players, managers and memorable moments all contribute to talking points. I've got lots of great memories from the game but a favourite involves one of my own heroes, the late Sir Bobby Robson. I'd just had a great face-to-face with the then Newcastle United manager and we were just leaving the building, chatting about his side's win earlier in the week, when he excused himself and walked up to two young girls. The girls instantly recognised everyone's favourite granddad of the time, but they hadn't bargained on him telling them how bad smoking was for their health. They immediately stubbed out their cigarettes.

Sir Bobby, ever the gent, rejoined me, apologised for his detour and we continued chatting like nothing had happened.

Enjoy this celebration of things good and bad from the beautiful game…

Colin Mitchell
June 2014

CHAPTER 1

AMAZING GAMES

EUROPEAN CHAMPIONS LEAGUE FINAL, MAY 2005
Liverpool 3 AC Milan 3 (Liverpool won 3-2 on penalties)

By halftime Liverpool were dead and buried in Istanbul. The hearts and hopes of the Reds' supporters had been shattered into tiny pieces. Their side was trailing 3-0 in the Champions League Final, the ultimate prize for European football clubs. The best the supporters could have hoped for in the second 45 minutes was to keep the score at a respectable level rather than suffer a totally demoralising rout. Even the most dedicated of fans from Anfield couldn't have dreamed of what would happen next…
In front of a 69,000 crowd in Istanbul's Ataturk Olympic Stadium, Milan had taken the lead in the first minute when defender Maldini volleyed home a free kick from Andrea Pirlo. Liverpool tried to fight back but just six minutes from halftime Crespo made it 2-0 when he latched onto a pass from Shevchenko. As the Reds attempted

to hold on for the halftime whistle so that they could formulate a battle plan for the second half, they were hit by a crippling third goal when Crespo chipped keeper Dudek to make it 3-0 with 60 seconds of the first period remaining.

Liverpool started the second half with German international Hamann coming off the substitutes' bench to replace defender Steve Finnan, a plan to boost midfield and push for a goal.

The half was just nine minutes old when captain Gerrard headed home a cross from Riise to make it 3-1. It might have looked like a consolation, but just two minutes later Liverpool had pulled the game back to 3-2.

Smicer, an early first-half substitute for injured Australian midfielder Kewell, fired the ball past Dida into the Milan goal and the most amazing of comebacks was on the cards. On the hour mark, Liverpool's battling captain Gerrard was fouled by Gattuso and the referee pointed to the penalty spot. Alonso's kick was saved, but the Spaniard scored from the rebound to bring the sides level at 3-3.

There were no further goals so the game went into extra time. Both sides failed to find the net in the next 30 minutes, which heralded a penalty shootout.

Serginho failed for Milan; Hamann scored. Pirlo failed to beat Dudek, Cisse scored; Tomasson hit the target but Riise failed. Kaka was successful, followed by Smicer. When Shevchenko's shot was stopped by Dudek, Liverpool's 3-2 shootout success was confirmed.

It was Liverpool's fifth victory in the competition and had come against all the odds.

TEAMS

AC Milan: Dida, Cafu, Paolo Maldini, Jaap Stam, Alessandro Nesta, Gennaro Gattuso (Rui Costa 112), Clarence Seedorf (Serginho 86), Andrea Pirlo, Kaka, Andriy Shevchenko, Hernan Crespo (Jon Dahl Tomasson 85). Unused subs: Christian Abbiati, Kakha Kaladze, Alessandro Costacurta, Vikash Dhorasoo. Manager: Carlo Ancelotti

Liverpool: Jerzy Dudek, Steve Finnan (Didi Hamann 46), Djimi Traore, Sami Hyypia, Jamie Carragher, John Arne Riise, Steven Gerrard, Luis Garcia, Xabi Alonso, Harry Kewell (Vladimir Smicer 23), Milan Baros (Djibril Cisse 85). Unused subs: Scott Carson, Josemi, Antonio Nunez, Igor Biscan. Manager: Rafa Benitez

A CAPTAIN'S PERFORMANCE

The extraordinary performance of midfielder and captain Steven Gerrard won the Man of the Match award. The lad born on Merseyside had always longed to lead out his local side in major finals and had been living the dream. But he had walked off the pitch at halftime to sink his head deep in his hands in the sanctuary of the dressing room, his dreams shattered. He would later admit that he thought the game was over. It is not a belief fans would have shared with Gerrard when they saw his amazing dedication to the second half.

Milan's 3-0 lead was the biggest halftime advantage any team had enjoyed in this competition's final.

As Gerrard held aloft the prized trophy there was speculation that he could be leaving Liverpool for Chelsea. But Gerrard hit back saying: 'How can I think of leaving Liverpool after a night like this? I am so happy to lift the cup for the fans. We were massive underdogs at the beginning of the competition and I'll put my hands up say and I didn't think we were going to go all the way.'

The London side came in with a £32 million bid for the player just weeks after the final, but they failed to lure Gerrard away from his beloved Liverpool.

AFTER THE FINAL WHISTLE…

'I've never seen anything like that. We were all deflated at halftime. We knew we had to get the next goal.' **Jamie Carragher, Liverpool defender**

'At halftime we knew we had to change things. You concede one goal in the first minute and it is very difficult, then we lose Harry Kewell. It was very difficult, but the players believed and won. Steven Gerrard is a key man, he has the mentality we want.' **Rafa Benitez, Liverpool manager**

'We had six minutes of madness in which we threw away the position we had reached until then. The match was well contested and it's inexplicable because the team played well for all 120 minutes. I think Milan played a marvellous final. We lost without deserving to lose and we have to accept our defeat.' **Carlo Ancelotti, AC Milan manager**

'It is very strange and hard to explain. It is a huge disappointment. I've had a few disappointments in my career but this is certainly among the major ones.' **Paolo Maldini, AC Milan captain.**

PREMIER LEAGUE, FEBRUARY 2011

Newcastle United 4 Arsenal 4

It was no surprise to see shattered supporters leaving the ground as Newcastle United trailed 4-0 at home to an Arsenal side that looked like they had the power to inflict a crushing defeat.

But those who departed early from St James' Park missed what was later labelled as the greatest Premier League comeback of all time.

The locals were already shattered by the £35 million record sale of striker Andy Carroll to Liverpool earlier in the week. And a succession of quick goals from the visitors had them fearing the worst.

Yet members of the Toon Army who did stay until the end nearly saw a remarkable victory and certainly did enjoy one of the most stunning goals of the season as their side earned an incredible draw.

With just 44 seconds on the referee's watch, Newcastle were a goal down and supporters had their heads in their hands. England forward Walcott had shown his lightning pace to beat the home defence and slot home the first.

A free kick from Arshavin after just three minutes found the head of Djourou for the second.

Walcott then turned provider for Holland striker van Persie with just ten minutes gone. The Dutchman headed his second after 26 minutes to give the Gunners a staggering early lead.

Those fans who liked a bet would probably have been wondering what sort of a cricket score they could get good odds on from the bookmakers.

But the halftime team talk turned the game on its head. A match that appeared to be over took on a whole new lease of life.

There were 50 minutes on the clock and Newcastle were still 4-0 down when Arsenal's Diaby was sent off for a double foul on Barton and Nolan. Some 18 minutes later, striker Koscielny brought down Best in the area and Barton scored from the penalty spot. Best then had a goal wrongly disallowed for offside before pulling another one back for Newcastle with 15 minutes to go.

Although some of the 51,500 fans had disappeared at the break, the noise from the home fans was rising and reached a staggering level when Newcastle were given another penalty, Koscielny adjudged to have pushed Williamson. Again it was despatched by Barton with just seven minutes remaining.

With the score line now 4-3 in favour of the visitors, it was the home side that looked the more determined and even capable of pulling off a massive shock. Defensive midfielder Tiote was the unlikely scorer, lashing home a goal of the season contender from outside of the area to bring the score level. Nolan even had a chance to win the game for Newcastle in the dying seconds, but by then the Geordie home fans were already starting their celebrations.

It was the first time any side had come back from four goals down to level the scores in a Premier League game.

TEAMS

Newcastle: Steve Harper, Fabricio Coloccini, Jose Enrique, Mike Williamson, Danny Simpson, Kevin Nolan, Joey Barton, Jonas Gutierrez, Cheick Tiote, Peter Lovenkrands (Nile Ranger 73), Leon Best (Danny Guthrie 89). Unused subs: Tim Krul, Sol Campbell, James Perch, Shane Ferguson, Michael Richardson. Manager: Alan Pardew

Arsenal: Wojciech Szczesny, Bacary Sagna, Laurent Koscielny, Johan Djourou (Sébastien Squillaci 48), Gael Clichy, Abou Diaby, Cesc Fabregas, Theo Walcott (Emmanuel Eboué 79), Jack Wilshere, Andrey Arshavin (Tomas Rosicky 69), Robin van Persie. Unused subs: Manuel Almunia, Kieran Gibbs, Marouane Chamakh, Nicklas Bendtner. Manager: Arsene Wenger

AFTER THE FINAL WHISTLE...

'When you're 4-0 down after 26 minutes and you haven't made a challenge you have to fear the worst, and I did. One of the most remarkable games I've been involved in, and I'm talking about 7-7 draws on Sunday mornings too.' **Alan Pardew, Newcastle manager**

'It is the greatest goal I've ever scored and the greatest moment of my career. Unbelievable. Incredible.' Cheick Tiote, Newcastle midfielder

'The sending-off was a turning point. We were hurt by going down to ten men. It had a psychological and physical impact. At 4-0 we were quite comfortable but we panicked a little bit.' **Arsene Wenger, Arsenal manager**

PREMIER LEAGUE, SEPTEMBER 2007

Portsmouth 7 Reading 4

Let's be honest: one of the most important things fans want to see at a football game is plenty of goals. But even the most dedicated supporter couldn't have expected the 11-goal thriller served up at Fratton Park between Portsmouth and Reading. And neither could they have predicted the amazing swings of fortune in a game that set a new aggregate best score for the Premier League.

With an England keeper at one end and a USA No.1 between the sticks at the other it was a game for international shot-stoppers to forget!

Portsmouth took the lead after just seven minutes through Benjani, who made it 2-0 30 minutes later; on the stroke of halftime Hunt pulled one back for Reading. With just three minutes of the second half gone, Kitson equalised for the visitors but seven minutes later Pompey were back in front through Hreidarsson.

Reading defender Shorey then had a penalty-kick saved by Pompey keeper James, after Diop had handled in the area. The game went 4-2 to the home side thanks to Benjani completing his hat trick on 70 minutes. It was 5-2 just five minutes later with a strike from Kranjcar.

Republic of Ireland striker Long entered the fray as a substitute just two minutes earlier and he pulled one back for the Royals on 79 minutes. But just two minutes later Davis made it 6-3. Supporters were still stunned by the nine goals they had seen but with two minutes of extra time on the clock Muntari made it 7-3 from the penalty spot after Kranjcar had been fouled by Rosenior.

Incredibly, the scoring still wasn't over! In the fourth minute of injury time, former England defender Campbell put through his own goal to complete the scoring. Shorey thought he had scored that final goal of the game but later lost the strike when it was ruled an own goal.

Some of the 20,102 fans had left the ground before the end of a pulsating game, which also had a number of near misses, terrific shots and a 'goal' that was ruled offside. The stats showed that Portsmouth had 63 percent of the possession; that there were 32 shots in total, 12 on target for Pompey, six for Reading; with nine off target for the home team and five for the visitors.

TEAMS

Portsmouth: David James, Glen Johnson, Sol Campbell, Sylvain Distin, Hermann Hreidarsson, Papa Bouba Diop, Sean Davis, Sulley Muntari, John Utaka, Benjani (David Nugent 80), Niko Kranjcar. Unused subs: Jamie Ashdown, Noe Pamarot, Matt Taylor, Pedro Mendes. Manager: Harry Redknapp

Reading: Marcus Hahnemann, Graeme Murty (Emerse Fae 77), Michael Duberry, Ivar Ingimarsson, Nicky Shorey, Liam Rosenior, Brynjar Gunnarsson (Shane Long

77), James Harper, Stephen Hunt, Kevin Doyle, Dave Kitson. Unused subs: Adam Federici, André Bikey, Leroy Lita. Manager: Steve Coppell

AFTER THE FINAL WHISTLE…

'It's difficult to analyse a match like that and if you try you will be there a very long time. We scored four goals away from home and had a chance for another with a penalty. We played a full part in the game. I don't think many teams will come here this season and score four.' **Steve Coppell, Reading manager**

'You play 4-5-1 – I thought I can't see them scoring, but we ended up with 11 goals. We were fantastic. I'd rather win 7-4 than 1-0. People have had a great day out today. They've seen goals, they've seen attacking football.' **Harry Redknapp, Portsmouth manager**

WORLD CUP FINAL, JULY 2006

Italy 1 France 1(Italy won 5-3 on penalties)

The biggest game on the planet in 2006 will forever be remembered as the World Cup Final in which Zinedine Zidane was sent off. It was the France legend's last game as a professional footballer and his red card meant that he not only missed the penalty shootout, which decided the outcome of the match, he was also banned from the professional game for life. Ironically, the midfielder had given France the lead in the seventh minute from the penalty spot after Italy defender Materazzi had conceded.

Materazzi then equalised in the 19th minute with a header from a Pirlo corner. The two players who had made such an impression in Berlin's Olympic Stadium were then involved in the controversial incident that led to Zidane's dismissal.

With the score still 1-1 in front of 69,000 fans at the end of 90 minutes the game had gone into extra time. Zidane looked as though he might have clinched the game five minutes into the second period of extra time with a header but keeper Buffon pushed the ball to safety.

Zidane and Materazzi were seen exchanging words as they jogged up the pitch close to each other—then the Frenchman suddenly turned and head-butted his opponent. The Italian fell to the ground and it was later revealed that the fourth official, using his radio headset, reported the incident to the referee. Zidane was sent from the pitch, the 14th red card of his career and his second at a World Cup tournament. He was only the fourth player to be dismissed from a World Cup Final and the first sent off in extra time.

Real Madrid star Zidane would have been a certainty to take one of France's spot-kicks in the penalty shootout, only the second time the method had been needed to decide the final. Pirlo gave France the lead in the shootout, Wiltord levelled; Materazzi was successful before Trezeguet hit the crossbar for France. Di Rossi scored for Italy, Abidal for France, then Del Piero for Italy and Sagnol for France before Grosso's match clincher.

Zidane, 34, had also created a more welcome piece of history, as he became only the fourth player to score three goals in World Cup Finals.

TEAMS

Italy: Gianluigi Buffon, Gianluca Zambrotta, Fabio Cannavaro, Marco Materazzi, Fabio Grosso, Gennaro Gattuso, Andrea Pirlo, Mauro Camoranesi (Alessandro Del Piero 86), Simone Perrotta (Daniele De Rossi 61), Francesco Totti (Vincenzo Iaquinta 61). Manager: Marcello Lippi
France: Fabien Barthez, Willy Sagnol, Lilian Thuram, William Gallas, Eric Abidal,

Patrick Vieira (Alou Diarra 56), Claude Makelele, Franck . (David Trezeguet 100), Zinedine Zidane, Florent Malouda, Thierry Henry (Sylvain Wiltord 107)Manager: Raymond Domenech

AFTER THE FINAL WHISTLE...

'After the match I realised that it [the red card] had been an enormous decision, thanks to the big media reaction to it. But right now, as I'm showing him the card, no. It's just a player on a team.' **Horacio Elizondo, match referee**

'I apologise to football, to the fans, to the team. After the game, I went into the dressing room and told them, "Forgive me. This doesn't change anything. But sorry everyone." But to him [Materazzi] I cannot. If I say sorry, I would also be admitting that what he himself did was normal. And for me it was not normal.' **Zinedine Zidane, France midfielder**

'Yes, I was tugging his shirt, but when he said to me scornfully, "If you want my shirt so much I'll give it to you afterwards", is that not a provocation? I answered that I'd prefer his sister, it's true. It's not a particularly nice thing to say, I recognise that. But loads of players say worse things. I didn't even know he had a sister before all this happened.' **Marco Materazzi, Italy defender**

PREMIER LEAGUE, SEPTEMBER 2001

Tottenham Hotspur 3 Manchester United 5

When you are 3-0 up at halftime—especially at home—you don't expect to finish the game with no points. But that is what happened to Tottenham when they came up against reigning champions Manchester United. Debut defender Richards, who had cost £8 million from Southampton, put Spurs ahead after 15 minutes with a close-range header from a Ziege corner.

Midfielder Poyet then chipped the ball over the United defence for star striker Ferdinand to hit home the second shortly afterwards.

A cheer erupted from the crowd every time a home player touched the ball, as free-flowing Spurs dominated, and it was again Poyet who set up the third goal, picking out Ziege who finished with a diving header. At the time, United boss Sir Alex Ferguson refused to say what he had said to his team during the break, although in later years he admitted he had told his side to go out, score early and see what happened.

United came out a different side for the second half and turned on the class. Despite being without suspended captain Roy Keane and injured Wales winger Ryan Giggs they took total control. The manager made two instant changes, bringing on Silvestre for Irwin and Solskjaer for Butt and just 60 seconds into the half United had pulled a goal back with a Cole header from a Beckham cross.

It was Beckham who then sent in a corner kick that was headed home by defender Blanc for a second and suddenly Spurs looked shaky. Holland striker van Nistelrooy scored the equaliser, also a header, but the fourth was a left-footed shot from Veron.

Then, three minutes from the end, Beckham added the fifth goal with a shot from his right foot just inside the penalty area. This went down as the game of the season and Sir Alex later classed it as one of his team's greatest comebacks, yet, surprisingly, the result gave them their first away points of that campaign.

TEAM

Tottenham: Neil Sullivan, Dean Richards, Ledley King, Chris Perry, Mauricio Taricco, Christian Ziege, Steffen Freund, Darren Anderton, Gus Poyet, Les Ferdinand,

Terry Sheringham. Subs: Kasey Keller, Sergei Rebrov, Alton Thelwell, Simon Davies, Matt Etherington. Manager: Glenn Hoddle

Man United: Fabien Barthez, Gary Neville, Denis Irwin, Ronny Johnsen, Laurent Blanc, David Beckham, Nicky Butt, Paul Scholes, Juan Sebastian Veron, Andy Cole, Ruud van Nistelrooy. Subs: Roy Carroll, Luke Chadwick, Ole Gunnar Solskjaer, Phil Neville, Mikael Silvestre. **Manager: Sir Alex Ferguson**

AFTER THE FINAL WHISTLE…

'A great game? I can't take much comfort from that because I've got to look at my own team and we're in the business of trying to win football matches. They [United] seem to be able to go up a few gears just when they want to. What went wrong? halftime!' **Glenn Hoddle, Tottenham manager**

'You could see Spurs deflate while we puffed ourselves up.' **Sir Alex Ferguson, Manchester United manager**

'It was awful. It was difficult to accept. I didn't want to leave the dressing room for one day, I wanted to hide in there.' **Gus Poyet, Tottenham midfielder**

PREMIER LEAGUE, APRIL 2009

Liverpool 4 Arsenal 4

Liverpool went into this match just a point behind leaders Manchester United, while Arsenal had suffered an FA Cup semi-final defeat to Chelsea the previous weekend. Russian forward Arshavin, not always flavour of the month with Gunners fans, put the visitors ahead after 36 minutes and, in a pulsating match which could have gone either way, he ended the night as Arsenal's point-saving hero.

Keeper Fabianski, who had come in for some tough criticism during the FA Cup game, turned around his own form and kept the home side at bay until three minutes after the break when Spain striker Torres equalised. And just eight minutes later Israel midfielder Benayoun put Liverpool ahead.

But Arshavin was a man on a mission and on 67 minutes blasted home a long-range effort to put Arsenal level. Less than three minutes later Arshavin had completed his hat trick and put the Gunners in front. But the applause from the visiting fans and groans from the Kop had hardly subsided before Torres hit his second of the evening to once again pull Liverpool level.

Arshavin was still determined to give his side something extra from the game and right on time he fired home his and Arsenal's fourth goal to make it 3-4. But this amazing game was still not over! In time added on and with almost the last kick of the match Benayoun grabbed his second goal to make it 4-4.

The result meant Arsenal had extended their unbeaten league run to 19 games and Liverpool went top of the Premier League on goal difference. Before this game Arshavin had scored just two goals since his arrival from Zenit Saint Petersburg for an Arsenal club record of £15m in January 2009. Not surprisingly he was named Man of the Match.

It was the first time he had scored four goals in a game and the first time since 1946 that a visiting player had scored that many in one game at Anfield. A crowd of more than 44,000 had witnessed an amazing goal scoring feat and watched one of the most entertaining Premier League games ever played.

TEAMS

Liverpool: Pepe Reina, Alvaro Arbeloa, Daniel Agger, Jamie Carragher, Fabio Aurelio, Javier Mascherano, Yossi Benayoun, Dirk Kuyt (El Zhar 86), Xabi Alonso,

Albert Riera (Ryan Babel 73), Fernando Torres. Unused subs: Andrea Dossena,
Lucas, David N'gog, Martin Skrtel, Diego Cavalieri. Manager: Rafael Benitez
Arsenal: Lukasz Fabianski, Bacary Sagna, Kolo Toure, Mikael Silvestre, Kieran
Gibbs, Denilson (Theo Walcott 65), Alex Song, Cesc Fabregas, Samir Nasri, Andrey
Arshavin, Nicklas Bendtner (Abou Diaby 89). Unused subs: Vito Mannone, Carlos
Vela, Eduardo, Aaron Ramsey, Emmanuel Eboue. Manager: Arsene Wenger

AFTER THE FINAL WHISTLE...

'Overall I believe that even if we were disappointed by the result we were not
disappointed by the performance. Liverpool played very well too. It was a game at a
frenetic pace of top quality technically and you could see both teams created many
chances.' **Arsene Wenger, Arsenal manager**

'The positive thing is we have scored four goals against Arsenal and it was a good
game. The other positive thing was the team fighting and working hard and we know
this has to be the way until the end of the season. We made massive mistakes. It is
difficult to explain because it was different players in different stages of the game.'
Rafael Benitez, Liverpool manager

PREMIER LEAGUE, AUGUST 2011

Manchester United 8 Arsenal 2

With the 2011–12 season just a few weeks old, reigning champions Manchester
United celebrated one of their best-ever Premier League victories. But for Arsenal the
8-2 humiliation at Old Trafford represented their worst defeat since 1986.

Even though the Gunners were hit by a number of injuries and suspensions,
manager Arsene Wenger could not escape the wrath of fans and critics for the manner

in which his side was destroyed. England striker Rooney ran the London side ragged as he scored a hat trick and Arsenal maintained the shocking statistic of not finishing any of their games so far that season with 11 men on the pitch.

The game was in its 22nd minute when Welbeck put the home side one up with a header from inside the penalty area. Arsenal had the chance to level the scores less than five minutes later when Evans fouled Walcott, but van Persie's penalty kick was saved by Spanish keeper de Gea.

Just over a minute later England winger Young smashed home a second for United from outside the box.

Injury meant Welbeck had to be substituted ten minutes before halftime, his place taken by Mexico striker Hernandez. With less than five of the first 45 minutes left on the clock, Young turned provider to set up Rooney, who fired in from outside of the area.

Just before the referee blew his whistle for the break, Walcott pulled one back for the visitors, firing low from inside the penalty box to make it 3-1 at halftime. But in the 64th minute Rooney grabbed his second and United's fourth, again assisted by Young and once again shooting from outside of the penalty area.

Less than three minutes later Rooney turned provider to lay on a chance for Nani lurking in the area to make it 5-1. With another three minutes on the clock Young was once again the creator, this time for Park to score from the edge of the box and make it 6-1.

On 73 minutes Arsenal's Holland striker van Persie snatched one back from close range to bring the score to 6-2 but any hopes the visitors had of a comeback were hit just three minutes later when defender Jenkinson picked up his second yellow card and was sent off.

Ten minutes to go and Walcott fouled Evra in the area to give United a penalty, which was converted by Rooney to complete his hat trick as United took the score to 7-2. Wales midfielder Giggs provided the pass for Young to complete the scoring in time added on.

The 75,448 crowd had witnessed an astonishing game that had seen United have 59 percent of the play and 25 shots, 15 on target, compared to Arsenal's 19 shots, 13 on target.

TEAMS

Manchester United: David de Gea, Patrice Evra, Phil Jones, Jonny Evans, Chris Smalling, Anderson (Ryan Giggs 68), Nani (Park Ji-sung 68), Ashley Young, Tom Cleverley, Wayne Rooney, Danny Welbeck (Javier Hernandez 35). Subs not used: Anders Lindegaard, Rio Ferdinand, Fabio da Silva, Dimitar Berbatov. Manager: Sir Alex Ferguson

Arsenal: Wojciech Szczesny, Laurent Koscielny, Johan Djourou, Carl Jenkinson, Armand Traore, Tomas Rosicky, Theo Walcott (Henri Lansbury 83), Aaron Ramsey, Andrey Arshavin, Francis Coquelin (Alex Oxlade-Chamberlain 62), Robin van Persie (Marouane Chamakh 83). Manager: Arsene Wenger

AFTER THE FINAL WHISTLE...

'You feel humiliated when you concede eight goals. It was a terrible day for us. It was a combination of an under-strength team and weakness. We had eight players out today. Anybody would suffer with eight players missing. We collapsed physically in the second half.' **Arsene Wenger, Arsenal manager**

'If you look at Arsenal the team is weakened—but we still did the job. We got careless at times and they made chances because they still have quality up front. But overall we are very satisfied that we kept the performance levels up.' **Sir Alex Ferguson, Manchester United manager**

'The performance today was incredible and we deserved the result. They had some players out but that should take nothing away from us. A lot of my milestone goals have come against Arsenal. My first goal when I was at Everton was against them and my first United goal in the Premier League came against them too.' **Wayne Rooney, Manchester United striker**

PREMIER LEAGUE, OCTOBER 2011

Manchester United 1 Manchester City 6

To lose any derby game is a disaster. To be hammered at home in a clash with your local rivals is something that is forever etched in history. But when that victory also keeps the winners at the top of the league it is even harder to swallow. When Man United were hit for six by Man City in this fixture it was their worst defeat at Old Trafford for 56 years. Ironically that earlier defeat, in 1955, was a 5-0 loss—also against City! To make matters worse, it was the first time in 81 years that the Red Devils had conceded six goals at home.

When Italy striker Balotelli put the visitors ahead with a shot into the bottom corner after 22 minutes United fans started to worry, although their fears eased when there were no more goals before halftime. The second period was almost one-way traffic with United's plight heightened when defender Evans was sent off just minutes into the second half for pulling down Balotelli.

With an hour gone England midfielder Milner put over a cross that Balotelli simply tapped in for his and City's second. Just nine minutes later Aguero made it

3-0 with an assist by Richards. Balotelli was subbed and his replacement Dzeko was almost instantly on the score sheet.

Scotland midfielder Fletcher pulled one back for United, a rasping shot from 20 years. But it was a false dawn for the home supporters.

With time almost out, Bosnia striker Dzeko finally got the goal he had been threatening and Spain midfielder Silva added a fifth. The sublime skills of Silva then laid on a second goal for Dzeko to ensure United's first home defeat since April 2010.

TEAMS

Manchester United: David De Gea, Patrice Evra, Rio Ferdinand, Johnny Evans, Chris Smalling, Anderson (Phil Jones 66), Nani (Javier Hernandez 65), Ashley Young, Darren Fletcher, Wayne Rooney, Danny Welbeck. Unused subs: Anders Lindegaard, Fabio da Silva, Park Ji-sung , Antonio Valencia, Dimitar Berbatov. Manager: Sir Alex Ferguson

Manchester City: Joe Hart, Micah Richards, Vincent Kompany, Joleon Lescott, Gael Clichy, James Milner (Aleksandar Kolarov 89), Gareth Barry, David Silva, Yaya Toure, Sergio Aguero (Samir Nasri 75), Mario Balotelli (Edin Dzeko 70). Unused subs: Costel Pantilimon, Pablo Zabaleta, Kolo Toure, Nigel de Jong.

AFTER THE FINAL WHISTLE…

'It's the worst result in my history. The impact will come from the embarrassment of the defeat. It was a horrible defeat but it was suicidal. Jonny Evans's sending off was a killer for us. I can't believe the score line. Even as a player I don't think I ever lost 6-1.' **Sir Alex Ferguson, Man United manager**

'I am satisfied because we beat United away. I don't think there are a lot of teams that can win here. This is important for our squad and I am happy for the three points, but in the end it is three points—we don't take six points.' **Roberto Mancini, Man City manager**

SECOND DIVISION, DECEMBER 1957

Charlton Athletic 7 Huddersfield Town 6

When your team is leading 5-1 away from home, playing against ten men and with less than half an hour left of the game you have every right to expect victory. But what should have happened and what did actually happen in 1957 left 12,535 fans at The Valley, home of Charlton Athletic, stunned.

Huddersfield, managed by Bill Shankly, were 1-5 up against the hosts who had lost their captain Ufton to injury—and this was in the days before substitutes. But the Terriers hadn't banked on Charlton left-winger Johnny Summers, who had changed his boots at halftime because they were falling apart!

Having already scored his side's first goal of the game he then hit FOUR more and created two others. Despite the fact that Howard made it 6-6 to the visitors, Ryan, who had already netted one goal, scored the winner with the last kick of the match—the goal coming from a cross by Summers!

The amazing result meant Huddersfield became the first league side to score six goals and still be the losing team. Summers had scored on 47, 64, 73, 78 and 81 minutes with Ryan netting on 63 and 89. Town scored through Massie on 27, Bain 35 and 49, McGarry pen 51, Ledger 62 and Howard 86.

TEAMS

Charlton: Willie Duff, Trevor Edwards, Don Townsend, John Hewie, Derek Ufton, Billy Kiernan, Ron White, Fred Lucas, Johnny Ryan, Stuart Leary, Johnny Summers.
Manager: Jimmy Trotter

Huddersfield: Sandy Kennon, Tony Conwell, Ray Wilson, Ken Taylor, Jack Connor, Bill McGarry, Bob Ledger, Stan Howard, Alex Bain, Les Massie, Ron Simpson.
Manager: Bill Shankly

AFTER THE FINAL WHISTLE...

'Things had not been coming off for Summers so I moved him from inside-left to centre-forward. As a last resort, I switched him to outside-left, his last chance to make good. How well he took it!' **Jimmy Trotter, Charlton manager**

'We were 5-1 up and we were still having a go. That was Shankly for you. Shankly was pacing up and down in the train [on the way home]. He was muttering to himself: "It's just one of those things. It's history".' **Ray Wilson, Huddersfield defender**

EUROPEAN CHAMPIONS LEAGUE FINAL, MAY 2012

Bayern Munich 1 Chelsea 1 (Chelsea won 4-3 on penalties)

If your last kick of the ball in your final game for a club results in victory in a major final, your hero status is guaranteed. But in truth Didier Drogba was already a Chelsea legend even before his winner against Bayern Munich gave the Blues their first-ever European Cup win.

The burly Ivory Coast striker hit 157 goals in 341 games for the Stamford Bridge side after joining them in summer 2004 for a then Chelsea record fee of £24 million.

But it was his double strike in the Champions League Final of 2012 before he left London for Shanghai Shenhua that would catapult him to true legendary status.

Bayern, playing in front of 62,500 fans in their home ground, the Allianz Arena in Munich, were favourites, having made the final for a ninth time and ending four of the games as champions.

Chelsea, who had lost out to English Premier League rivals Manchester United in 2008, were competing in only their second final.

Bayern were undoubtedly the more dangerous side and a shot from Robben was pushed onto his sticks by keeper Cech and another from the Holland striker was blocked by Cahill. With seven minutes to go Chelsea's resolve was finally broken when a cross from Kroos was headed into the ground by Muller and the ball bounced over the keeper.

It was then the turn of Drogba to live up to his cult status among Chelsea fans when, just five minutes later, he latched onto a corner from Mata and headed an equaliser to take the game to extra time. But hero turned to villain when Drogba fouled France winger Ribery in the box to give Bayern a penalty.

Robben had the chance to win the game with the spot-kick but his shot was weak and saved by Cech. There were no more goals and so the game went to a penalty shootout. Lahm gave Bayern the lead despite the keeper just touching the shot.

Mata's attempt was saved by keeper Neuer before Gomez made it 2-0 to the Germans. Luiz pulled one back with a shot into the top of the net then Neuer himself made it 3-1.

Chelsea veteran Lampard thundered in his side's second before a Cech save from Olic.

Full back Cole drew Chelsea level at 3-3 and then saw Schweinsteiger's attempt pushed to safety by Cech.

That meant if Drogba could score with the next penalty kick his parting gift to Chelsea would be the European Cup. He sent the keeper the wrong way with a shot into the bottom corner to cap a performance that made him the official Man of the Match. Chelsea had been without their suspended captain John Terry, who was sent off in the semi-final against Barcelona. He still donned his full kit to take part in the celebrations and lift the European Cup, despite Lampard being skipper on the day.

Four years earlier Terry had missed a spot-kick in the penalty shootout failure that cost his side victory against Manchester United in the Champions League Final of 2008. For boss Di Matteo, who had taken over as Chelsea's interim manager just two months earlier, it was a second trophy in two weeks, having won the FA Cup with victory over Liverpool.

TEAMS

Bayern Munich: Manuel Neuer, Philipp Lahm, Jerome Boateng, Anatoliy Tymoshchuk, Diego Contento, Bastian Schweinsteiger, Toni Kroos, Arjen Robben, Thomas Muller (Daniel van Buyten 87), Franck Ribéry (Ivica Olic 97), Mario Gomez. Unused subs: Hans-Jorg Butt, Rafinha, Takashi Usami, Danijel Pranjic, Nils Petersen. Manager: Jupp Heynckes

Chelsea: Petr Cech, José Bosingwa, Gary Cahill, Ashley Cole, John Obi Mikel, Frank Lampard, Salomon Kalou (Fernando Torres 84), Juan Mata, Ryan Bertrand (Florent Malouda 73), Didier Drogba. Unused subs: Ross Turnbull, Paulo Ferreira, Michael Essien, Oriol Romeu, Daniel Sturridge. Manager: Roberto Di Matteo

AFTER THE FINAL WHISTLE...

'I believe a lot in destiny. I pray a lot. It was written a long time ago. God is wonderful. This team is amazing.' **Didier Drogba, Chelsea striker**

'We have a group of players that have a big heart, passion, motivation and desire. That was the only way to be able to achieve this trophy. Bayern is a good team and when they scored there was not much time left. Games like this need passion and players who rise to the occasion.' **Roberto Di Matteo, Chelsea manager**

'We must blame ourselves for having so many opportunities without profiting. When you score in the 83rd minute you need to keep that lead, then we had a penalty in extra time. Penalties are a lottery, we know that from history.' **Juup Heynckes, Bayern Munich manager**

PREMIER LEAGUE, FEBRUARY 1999

Nottingham Forest 1 Manchester United 8

The stunning score line hid the real story behind the match—substitute Ole Gunnar Solskjaer scored four of Manchester United's goals! The Norway striker had taken to the pitch with just 18 minutes remaining and in the final ten minutes of the game became the first sub to hit four in a Premier League game.

The player nicknamed the 'baby-faced assassin' hadn't been expected to make an appearance, as the Red Devils were already 4-1 up. And as he entered the fray he had been instructed to pass the ball around as the team saw out the game!

In a frantic start to the fixture Yorke gave United the lead after just two minutes, following a Beckham corner knocked on by Scholes. Just four minutes later Forest were level through Rodgers. And just 60 seconds after that Cole latched onto a long ball from the back by Stam and rounded the keeper to make it 2-1 to the visitors, which is how the score stayed until after halftime.

Cole added his second five minutes into the second period and Yorke completed his double on 67. Five minutes later Yorke was replaced by Solskjaer. With ten minutes left Gary Neville crossed for the sub to tap in his first. Eight minutes later Solskjaer was put through by Beckham to score his second. With the game virtually over, Scholes fed Solskjaer a pass that he hit on the volley to complete his hat trick. In injury time Butt passed to the Norwegian in the penalty area and he got his fourth goal.

The victory, in front of a 30,000 crowd, meant United stayed at the top of the league and Forest were still rooted to the foot of the table. Solskjaer, whose four goals came in the space of 12 minutes—which included injury time—did not win the Man of the Match award, which went to Beckham.

TEAMS

Nottingham Forest: Dave Beasant, John Harkes, Craig Armstrong (Hugo Porfirio 74), Jon Olav Hjelde, Alan Rogers, Steve Stone, Carlton Palmer, Andy Johnson, Scot Gemmill (Jesper Mattsson 57), Pierre van Hooijdonk, Jean-Claude Darcheville (Dougie Freedman 26). Unused subs: Mark Crossley, Chris Bart-Williams. Manager: Ron Atkinson

Manchester United: Peter Schmeichel, Gary Neville, Ronny Johnsen, Jaap Stam, Phil Neville, David Beckham, Paul Scholes, Roy Keane (John Curtis 72), Jesper Blomqvist (Nicky Butt 86), Dwight Yorke (Ole Gunnar Solskjaer 72), Andy Cole. Unused subs: Raimond van der Gouw, David May. Manager: Sir Alex Ferguson

AFTER THE FINAL WHISTLE...

'To be honest I was sitting there thinking I wasn't going on because Andy [Cole] and Dwight [Yorke] were on fire. Then the manager just said, "Ole get changed". Jim Ryan [the coach] had a few famous words like play it nice and simple as we don't need any more goals, but of course I don't like to do it that way, do I?' **Ole Gunnar Solskjaer, Man United striker**

'If I ever feel guilty about the teams I pick, it invariably centres around him [Solskjaer]. He really deserves better. But the fact is he is better than anyone else at the club as a substitute. He can come on and not be disturbed by it; he finds the flow easily.' **Sir Alex Ferguson, Man United manager**

'Did Solskjaer score four? It's a good job they didn't bring him on earlier. In a nutshell, we were murdered by a magnificent side. We contributed a bit to the entertainment but we didn't play as well as we could.' **Ron Atkinson, Forest manager**

EUROPEAN CHAMPIONS LEAGUE FINAL, MAY 1999

Manchester United 2 Bayern Munich 1

Already crowned English Premier League champions and winners of the FA Cup, Manchester United went into the European Cup final looking to complete a unique treble.

But it was Bayern, having won the Bundesliga and earned a place in Germany's cup final, which took the lead.

Until the dying seconds of the game it looked highly likely that an early goal from Basler had sealed victory for the Germans. But in an amazing end to the game United scored twice in injury time—one from each of their two substitutes—to seal what was an incredible victory.

Basler curled home a free kick from just outside of the penalty area after just six minutes to put his side ahead in Barcelona's Camp Nou stadium, in front of 90,000 spectators.

With captain Roy Keane and influential England midfielder Paul Scholes both missing the final through suspension, victory was always going to be a difficult ask for the Red Devils and although they fought hard they carved out few attempts in the first half.

With the Germans looking strong in the second period United boss Ferguson brought on England forward Sheringham and with just ten minutes to go sent on the man who had become known as the side's 'super sub', Norway striker Solskjaer.

Jancker hit the crossbar for Bayern before both of United's subs tested Germany keeper Kahn.

As the fourth official held up the board to indicate three minutes of injury time United won a corner that Bayern failed to clear. After a shot from Giggs failed, the ball then fell to Sheringham who right-footed home.

It looked like the game would go to extra time. But just 30 seconds after United's goal they got another corner. England midfielder Beckham was once again the man who took the set piece and this time the ball fell to Sheringham who nodded down for Solskjaer to hit the winner into the roof of the net. United's goals had come so late in the game that officials had already tied ribbons in Bayern's colours to the trophy ready for the presentation!

For Schmeichel, stand-in captain for the evening, it was a fitting end to his career with Manchester United. Bayern returned home stunned, and suffered further heartbreak when they lost their domestic cup final.

TEAMS

Manchester United: Peter Schmeichel, Gary Neville, Ronny Johnsen, Jaap Stam, Denis Irwin, Ryan Giggs, David Beckham, Nicky Butt, Jesper Blomqvist (Teddy Sheringham 67), Dwight Yorke, Andy Cole (Ole Gunnar Solskjaer 81). Unused subs: Raimond van der Gouw, David May, Phil Neville, Wes Brown, Jonathan Greening Manager: Sir Alex Ferguson

Bayern Munich: Oliver Kahn, Lothar Matthaus (Thorsten Fink 80), Markus Babbel, Thomas Linke, Samuel Kuffour, Michael Tarnat, Stefan Effenberg, Mario Basler (Hasan Salihamidzic 90), Carsten Jancker, Alexander Zickler (Mehmet Scholl 71). Unused subs: Bernd Dreher, Thomas Helmer, Thomas Strunz, Ali Daei Manager: Ottmar Hitzfeld

AFTER THE FINAL WHISTLE...

'To lose a final is always hard, especially this way. Tonight it was not the best team that won but the luckiest. It's bitter, sad and unbelievable. We're all disappointed. You can't blame the team. We had the match in control for 90 minutes. We had bad luck, hitting the post and the crossbar.' **Lothar Matthaus, Bayern Munich and Germany midfielder**

'I feel so sorry for my team because they were so close to winning this match. It's really difficult to digest and this is inconceivable for us but then this is what football is all about. Normally when the opposition equalise you are expecting extra time and it was a shock to our team when they scored the winner two minutes later. It could take days or even weeks to recover from this.' **Ottmar Hitzfeld, Bayern Munich manager**

'My players never give in. You always expect they can do something. But this time I thought we were beaten. It's very difficult to describe how I feel just now but if anyone still wonders why I stayed at Man United they can see here why. You can talk about tactics all you like but that spirit is unbeatable at times. Tonight they just never gave in.' **Sir Alex Ferguson, Man United manager**

'I had a premonition I was going to do something that night. I was concentrating on playing half an hour extra in a Champions League final, this was something I was going to savour. But I ruined that. I had this run and I scored. I cannot remember what I was thinking. I was just sliding, celebrating.' **Ole Gunnar Solskjaer, Man United and Norway striker**

PREMIER LEAGUE, APRIL 1996

Liverpool 4 Newcastle United 3

For those who witnessed this seven-goal thriller at Anfield it was a game never to be forgotten.

Along with the millions who also watched on live television around the world it was a match that would be etched in their memories forever. Football fans later voted it the match of the decade, as part of the first ten years of the Premier League.

Newcastle went into the game noted for an attacking style that had led to them being nicknamed the 'Entertainers', for their cavalier style of football. Their problems lay at the back, where the club's defence often left a lot to be desired. Nevertheless, under boss Kevin Keegan their aim was to score as many goals as they could!

The Geordies were lying second in the league and victory would have taken them to the top with Manchester United, and with games in hand. The visitors' hopes were shattered after just two minutes when Fowler put the Reds ahead with a header from a

Redknapp cross for his 27th goal of the season.

Then Newcastle stunned the 40,702 crowd just eight minutes later when England striker Ferdinand equalised after receiving a ball from Colombia forward Asprilla. Four minutes later France winger Ginola put United ahead with a great solo effort.

Fowler got his second of the game ten minutes into the second half, set up this time by McManaman. But Liverpool were level for just two minutes before Asprilla made it 3-2, thanks to a pass from midfield general Lee.

England striker Collymore brought the scores level once more after 68 minutes and as an action-packed game neared its end it looked like Newcastle would leave Merseyside with a draw.

With two minutes added time on the clock Collymore struck again to make it 4-3 after getting a through ball from Barnes.

Liverpool celebrated as their team took the spoils, and the abiding memory from television coverage was the image of Newcastle boss Keegan, a former Anfield favourite, slumped over the advertising hoardings in disbelief at the result. Amazingly, almost exactly a year later there was a repeat of the 4-3 score line between the two sides at Liverpool, although the game was nowhere near as exciting despite the fact that Liverpool took a 3-0 lead and clinched the game in time added on.

TEAMS

Liverpool: David James, Mark Wright (Steve Harkness 45), John Scales, Neil Ruddock, Jason McAteer, Jamie Redknapp, John Barnes, Rob Jones (Ian Rush 85), Steve McManaman, Stan Collymore, Robbie Fowler. Unused sub: Tony Warner. Manager: Roy Evans

Newcastle United: Pavel Srnicek, Steve Watson, Steve Howey (Darren Peacock 82), Philippe Albert, John Beresford, Peter Beardsley, David Batty, Robert Lee, David Ginola, Faustino Asprilla, Les Ferdinand. Unused subs: Keith Gillespie, Lee Clark. Manager: Kevin Keegan

AFTER THE FINAL WHISTLE...

'There was so much around this game, in terms of suspense, which made it so emotive for the fans in the stands and the people watching on TV. If I was supporting either of the teams I would have been jumping to my feet every single second. The fans said that it was an amazing game to watch and it was just great to be there. To see Liverpool scoring the winning goal was such a frustration for everyone close to the club.' **David Ginola, Newcastle and France winger**

'Managers would be dead within six months if every game was like that. That was kamikaze football. Great for the fans but realistically nobody will win the championship defending every week like these teams did tonight.' **Roy Evans, Liverpool manager**

FA CUP THIRD ROUND, JANUARY 1991

West Bromwich Albion 2 Woking 4

The FA Cup's third round is noted for springing shock results. But few were expecting this humiliation of Albion, especially by a player more noted for his cricket-playing abilities! Division Two West Brom were four tiers higher than Woking in England's football pyramid and this is one result that really should not have happened.

It wasn't just a freak result by the Isthmian League side. The non-leaguers deserved their victory. And Tim Buzaglo earned his status as hero of the moment. Some 5,000 fans—almost the capacity of the Cardinals' home ground—travelled with the Surrey side to the Midlands to witness what was an amazing result at The Hawthorns in front of a 14,000 crowd.

Even the home fans were quick to acknowledge just how great an achievement had been pulled off as they raced onto the pitch to carry Buzaglo shoulder high and called on their club to sign him on the spot! Amazingly, the visitors were 1-0 down at halftime to a West header and there wasn't a hint of the drama to come in the second period.

Up stepped Buzaglo—an international cricketer for Gibraltar!— who scored a hat trick in a 15-minute spell. And then substitute Worsfold added a fourth. Bradley hit Albion's second consolation goal in the dying stages.

Former Arsenal midfielder Brian Talbot was sacked as Albion boss shortly after this defeat, while Geoff Chapple, the Woking gaffer, led his team to the next round where they were defeated just 1-0 by the mighty Everton.

TEAMS

West Brom: Melvyn Rees; Craig Shakespeare, Graham Harvey, Graham Roberts, Darren Bradley, Gary Strodder, Tony Ford, Colin West, Gary Bannister, Bernard McNally, Gary Robson. Subs: Les Palmer, Simeon Hodson. Manager: Brian Talbot
Woking: Tim Read, Stewart Mitchell, Adie Cowler, Bradley Pratt, Trevor Baron, Shane Wye, Dereck Brown, Mark Biggins, Mark Franks, Tim Buzaglo, Lloyd Wye. Substitutes: Terry Worsfold, Andy Russell. Manager: Geoff Chapple.

AFTER THE FINAL WHISTLE...

'I remember looking in the West Brom dressing room and their players were just sitting around as casual as you like, reading the newspapers. I thought to myself, "who the hell are we?" At halftime we were 1-0 down but that was all right because all I wanted was for us to give a good account of ourselves for us and the league. Then we went 4-1 up and I remember people telling me later how they switched on their radios back in Woking to find out there had been another goal.' **Geoff Chapple, Woking manager**

'We deserved to win it. It was funny coming out of the dressing room because I asked a ball boy what the score would be and he said "5-0 to Albion".' **Tim Buzaglo, Woking's hat trick hero**

EUROPEAN CUP FINAL, MAY 1960

Real Madrid 7 Eintracht Frankfurt 3

There was a record crowd, the highest aggregate score and a fifth European Cup victory in a row for Real Madrid. The European Cup Final of 1960, watched by a crowd at Scotland's Hampden Park recorded at 127,600, but in some places suggested to be as high as 134,000, really was a memorable match.

Eintracht Frankfurt might not have even taken part in the showdown had it not been for the legendary Puskas issuing an apology before the final. Puskas had alleged that the West German team had used drugs in their 1954 World Cup victory over his native Hungary.

As a result, the German Football Association banned any of their sides from facing a team containing the player. Puskas relented with a written apology before the European Cup Final—and then went on to hit four goals for Madrid against the Germans!

The goal-fest should have come as no surprise as Madrid had gone into the game with a history of attacking and scoring, compared to the more defensive nature of their opponents. Frankfurt took the lead against the run of play after just 18 minutes through a Kress header. But after 22 minutes Di Stéfano equalised with a tap-in and just three minutes later got his second, another easy-to-score effort.

Puskas got the first of his goals just before halftime and then completed his haul of four in the 56th, 60th and 71st minutes. His second goal came from the penalty spot and then he completed his hat trick with a header, before a long-range rocket completed his record-breaking tally.

Stein hit two goals in under three minutes, 72 and 75, one either side of the goal that completed the hat trick for Di Stéfano.

The Germans, who were making their European debut, faced a Real Madrid side who were the undisputed kings of Europe. And even the neutral fans in the stadium had to cheer the Spanish team as they completed a lap of honour.

For manager Munoz, who was in his first season as coach, it was the first of two European Cup wins. He also won the trophy three times as a midfielder with Madrid—the first person to lift the cup as both a player and manager. He went on to manage Madrid for 13 years and also won nine league titles before becoming Spain's national team coach.

TEAMS

Real Madrid: Rogelio Dominguez, Marquitos, José Santamaria, Pachin, José Maria Vidal, José Maria Zarraga, Canario, Luis del Sol, Alfredo Di Stéfano, Ferenc Puskas,

Francisco Gento. Manager: Miguel Munoz

Eintracht Frankfurt: Egon Loy, Friedel Lutz, Hermann Hofer, Hans Weilbacher,

Hans-Walter Eigenbrodt, Dieter Stinka, Richard Kress, Dieter Lindner, Erwin Stein,

Alfred Pfaff, Erich Meier. Manager: Paul Osswald

AFTER THE FINAL WHISTLE...

'We were 1-0 up already and about to score again. Most of the Scots in the stands were on our side. Then they scored two, three quick goals which could have been avoided. We didn't defend good enough there. But you have to admit, that was the best team at that time, they were excellent, their football was indeed world class.'

Alfred Pfaff, Eintracht captain

'It was a fair game, best of which were the German Richard Kress and the Scottish crowd. The penalty for us would have never been one in Spain, but what should I do? Football is my job and so I had the duty to score a goal from it. This is the happiest day of my life.' **Ferenc Puskas, Real Madrid forward**

FA CUP FINAL, MAY 1988

Wimbledon 1 Liverpool 0

It was the former non-league side versus the reigning champions of England. There could be only one winner...or so the pundits believed! But The Dons, a Football League side for just 11 years, hadn't risen from the lower regions of England's football pyramid to the top-flight, then Division One, without a special kind of team spirit and bond.

The Dons had often been accused of being a physical side but the truth was that they also had some players with real skill. They certainly had a side with determination. Liverpool were determined to become the first team to win a league and FA Cup double for a second time—but the final ended in total disaster for the Reds.

Not only did they lose to Wimbledon, but their deadly striker Aldridge became the first player to miss a penalty in the Cup Final. Dons' keeper Beasant became the first shot-stopper to captain a side in this final and also the first to save a spot-kick. More than 98,000 supporters were inside the old Wembley Stadium for the match, which was played in brilliant sunshine. And it was a goal after just 37 minutes that put the lights out for Liverpool.

Wise took a free kick, which Sanchez headed into the net. Liverpool had a goal by Beardsley disallowed because the referee had already blown up for a free kick. The missed penalty came an hour into the game—and the fact it was saved was fortunate as television replays showed the spot-kick should not have been awarded in the first place.

It was the first missed penalty kick in 12 attempts by Republic of Ireland striker Aldridge.

Wimbledon, the side they had dubbed the Crazy Gang, lifted their first major trophy, the only major cup they ever won: in 2004 they moved out of London and became MK Dons. As English teams were banned from European competition until 1990–91 because of the 1985 Heysel Stadium disaster, which had involved Liverpool, Wimbledon were not allowed to compete in the European Cup Winners' Cup.

Liverpool gained slight revenge when they beat Wimbledon 2-1 a few months later in the Charity Shield, the curtain opener for the new season.

TEANS

Wimbledon: Dave Beasant, Clive Goodyear, Eric Young, Andy Thorn, Terry Phelan, Alan Cork (Laurie Cunningham 56), Vinnie Jones, Lawrie Sanchez, Dennis Wise, John Fashanu, Terry Gibson (John Scales 63). Manager: Bobby Gould

Liverpool: Bruce Grobbelaar, Steve Nichol, Gary Gillespie, Alan Hansen, Gary Ablett, Ray Houghton, Nigel Spackman (Jan Molby 74), Steve McMahon, John Barnes, Peter Beardsley, John Aldridge (Craig Johnston 64). Manager: Kenny Dalglish

AFTER THE FINAL WHISTLE...

'We were the Cinderellas of the FA Cup. For the winning goal, Wisey curls it in, Sanchez gets a near-post header and all you can see is red shirts, they couldn't defend it.' **Bobby Gould, Wimbledon manager**

'It was a sea of red for Liverpool, and there was this blue section, I'm sure our fans were outnumbered four, five to one in the stadium, but they never stopped singing all the way through. I played in the third round at Wealdstone as a non-league player, and it was massive for us then. A couple of years later, there I was beating the mighty Liverpool.' **Vinnie Jones, Wimbledon midfielder**

PREMIER LEAGUE, OCTOBER 1996

Newcastle United 5 Manchester United 0

Newcastle had thrown away a massive 12-point lead to lose the previous season's title to Manchester United. But they had stunned their rivals during the summer break by beating them to the signature of England striker Alan Shearer.

The Geordie had moved to his hometown club from Blackburn Rovers for a then world record fee of £15 million and he was to play a major part in a crushing and shock defeat for the Red Devils.

France winger Ginola started the rout when he put over a corner, which unlikely scorer Peacock, a central defender, headed home after just 12 minutes during a goalmouth scramble.

Ginola added a second on the half hour to make it 2-0 to the home side at the break. Shearer was the provider for fellow striker Ferdinand to head home a third on 62 and then scored the fourth himself 12 minutes later. But the most memorable goal that made it 5-0 to the Geordies came from another central defender—fans' favourite Albert—with just seven minutes to go.

The Belgian created his own space and then chipped Man United's highly rated Denmark keeper Schmeichel to send the home crowd into raptures. Boss Keegan stunned supporters again just a few months later when he resigned. But it was no surprise that this game was named in the shortlist of ten of the best games of the first 20 years of the Premier League.

Man United went on to retain the league title, with Newcastle runners-up to Ferguson's side for a second successive season.

TEAMS

Newcastle United: Pavel Srnicek, Steve Watson (Warren Barton 87), John Beresford, Philippe Albert, Darren Peacock, David Batty, Rob Lee (Lee Clark 87), Peter Beardsley, David Ginola, Alan Shearer, Les Ferdinand. Subs not used: Shaka Hislop, Tino Asprilla, Keith Gillespie. Manager: Kevin Keegan. Manchester United: Peter Schmeichel, Gary Neville, Denis Irwin, David May, Gary Pallister, Karel Poborsky (Brian McClair 66), David Beckham, Ronny Johnsen (Paul Scholes 66), Nicky Butt,

Ole Gunnar Solskjaer (Jordi Cruyff 56), Eric Cantona. Subs not used: Raimond Van der Gouw, Phil Neville. Manager: Sir Alex Ferguson

AFTER THE FINAL WHISTLE...

'Kevin Keegan went for broke with an attacking team. He loved to see all-out attack, often to his downfall, but when it came off it was spectacular to watch. This was payback time, which made it even sweeter. It would have been difficult for anyone to live with us that day.' **Alan Shearer, Newcastle United striker**

'We ripped them apart. We wanted revenge and got it. That Newcastle side was one of the greats. We had a lot of players who could really pass well and were able to go past people. We were also all extremely fit and scored goals from all over the pitch.' **Rob Lee, Newcastle United midfielder**

CHAMPIONSHIP PLAY-OFF FINAL, MAY 2008

Bristol City 0 Hull City 1

The writer of a fairy story couldn't have dreamed up a better ending to this clash at Wembley in front of 86,700 fans. Hull-born Dean Windass, 39, who had returned to the club just over a year earlier, scored the only goal of the game to put the Tigers into the top-flight of English football for the first time ever.

In the play-off semi-final Windass had scored one of the goals that had beaten Watford, the other in the 2-0 victory coming from Barmby, who was also born in Hull. Having just missed out on the two automatic promotion places to the Premier League by finishing third in the Championship, Hull faced the Robins in the final. The team had finished one place below them.

The Tigers would have gone up automatically if they had won their final day fixture against Ipswich. Instead they had to fight it out in a match that many rate as the most valuable fixture on the English domestic calendar, at that time worth around £60 million to the victors. The winners enjoy the benefits of Premier League prize money, television revenue and enhanced sponsorships.

Windass scored the only goal of the game after 38 minutes, with a spectacular 20-yard volley into the top corner of the net. He was substituted with just less than 20 minutes of the match remaining. His side came under some heavy pressure late in the game and even had to clear a Trundle shot off the line in the dying minutes.

Hull survived in the Premier League for the next two seasons before relegation at the end of 2009–10. Bristol City remained in the Championship until the end of 2012–13 when they were relegated to League One.

TEAMS

Bristol City: Adriano Basso, Bradley Orr (Lee Johnson 45), Louis Carey, Liam Fontaine, James McAllister, David Noble (Ivan Sproule 63), Marvin Elliott, Nick Carle (Darren Byfield 76), Michael McIndoe, Dele Adebola, Lee Trundle. Unused subs: Chris Weale, Tamas Vasko. Manager: Gary Johnson. Hull City: Boaz Myhill, Sam Ricketts, Wayne Brown, Michael Turner, Andy Dawson, Richard Garcia, Ian Ashbee, Bryan Hughes, Nick Barmby (Craig Fagan 67), Fraizer Campbell (Dean Marney 90), Dean Windass (Caleb Folan 71). Unused subs: Matt Duke, Nathan Doyle. Manager: Phil Brown.

AFTER THE FINAL WHISTLE...

'It feels unbelievable. I don't think there is anyone left in Hull today, looking at how many supporters we've got here. To score the wining goal is fantastic. We've worked hard from the start of the season and we've got our rewards.' **Dean Windass, Hull City striker**

'It is very fitting that Dean Windass got the winning goal. The players have tried hard all season and thoroughly deserve it. It is a fantastic feeling to do it here in front of all of these supporters.' **Phil Brown, Hull City manager**

'We got beaten and all I can say is well done to Hull. We had a few half chances and we weren't at our best. The game could have gone either way but for a bit of experienced play from Dean Windass. We had as many chances but didn't take them and Dean Windass is a clever player like that. We threw our kitchen sink at them at the end but it didn't come off.' **Gary Johnson, Bristol City manager**

PREMIER LEAGUE, OCTOBER 2008

Arsenal 4 Tottenham Hottspur 4

Some 60,000 fans were in a sold-out Emirates Stadium to see an amazing North London derby that wasn't decided until the final seconds of injury time. In a game that see-sawed one way and then another it was Spurs who were celebrating most thanks to two late, late goals, including a last-gasp equaliser from England winger Lennon.

Tottenham had silenced the home crowd when they took the lead through former Arsenal midfielder Bentley after 13 minutes: a stunning 40-yard volley. With just eight minutes of the first half remaining a van Persie corner was headed home by Silvestre for the equaliser. And just one minute into the second period van Persie provided the cross for defender Gallas to head a second and make it 2-1.

On 64 minutes that score became 3-1 when Nasri put the ball over keeper Gomes, and Adebayor raced onto the ball to stab it home. Substitute Bent was on hand to pull one back for the visitors just three minutes later. Keeper Almunia couldn't hold a shot from Huddlestone and the England striker fired home the rebound.

Just one minute later Arsenal had restored their advantage when Dutchman van Persie got on the score sheet himself with a piledriver to make it 4-2. With just a minute plus injury time left on the clock it looked like Arsenal were going to be North London's top guns. But England midfielder Jenas dragged them back to 4-3 with 60 seconds left on the clock.

And then, as the referee counted down the remaining seconds of four minutes of injury time, a Modric shot was deflected onto the post and Lennon fired home the rebound for an unlikely 4-4 draw. It was only the second game for which Redknapp had been manager of Spurs, following his departure from Portsmouth. Despite his side dropping points at home Arsenal striker van Persie was named Man of the Match.

TEAMS

Arsenal: Manuel Almunia, Bacary Sagna, Mikael Silvestre, William Gallas, Gael Clichy, Theo Walcott (Emmanuel Eboue 75), Cesc Fabregas, Denilson, Samir Nasri (Alex Song 88), Robin van Persie (Diaby 81), Emmanuel Adebayor. Unused subs: Lukasz Fabianski, Kolo Toure, Carlos Vela, Nicklas Bendtner. Manager: Arsene Wenger.

Tottenham: Heurelho Gomes, Alan Hutton (Chris Gunter 79), Vedran Corluka, Jonathan Woodgate, Benoit Assou-Ekotto, David Bentley, Luka Modric, Jermaine Jenas, Tom Huddlestone, Gareth Bale (Aaron Lennon 55), Roman Pavlyuchenko (Darren Bent 65). Unused subs: César, Didier Zokora, Fraizer Campbell, Jamie O'Hara. Manager: Harry Redknapp

AFTER THE FINAL WHISTLE…

'It was a real old-fashioned slugging match. We went for it and then they went for it. It really was an amazing game of football to be involved in. We gave away some bad goals, from set pieces too, even though we worked hard on that on Tuesday at training.' **Harry Redknapp, Tottenham manager**

'We are very angry and disappointed but on the other hand we have to stay positive because we were two levels above and produced an outstanding game. My team produced an outstanding performance and deserved to win, but maybe we wanted it too much and put ourselves under pressure rather than scoring goals five and six. What happened to us when we were leading 4-2 should never happen.' **Arsene Wenger, Arsenal manager**

SERIES A, MAY 2001

Inter Milan 0 AC Milan 6

It's got to be one of the most intriguing derby games in the world—AC Milan vs. Inter Milan—with both sides having the San Siro Stadium as their home ground! Milan's 6-0 defeat of Inter in 2001 is the biggest thrashing handed out in the showdown.

Highly rated referee Pierluigi Collina came in for stick over some of his decisions in this game but there is no doubt the Nerazzurri was outclassed. Comandini scored two first-half goals—his only strikes in domestic competition for Milan—for a 2-0 lead at the break. Giunti then scored his only goal for the club, after 53 minutes, before Shevchenko headed in the fourth after 66 and tapped in a fifth 11 minutes later. Man of the Match Serginho completed the route nine minutes from time in front of a 78,000 crowd.

Going into this Derby della Madonnina both sides had been on the same number of points in the Serie A table but that was not reflected by the action on the pitch. Years later Rossoneri fans still talk about this victory over their rivals, one that generated countless jokes and television sketches. The two sides played out a 2-2 draw in their other clash that season.

TEAMS

Inter Milan: Sebastien Frey, Matteo Ferrari, Laurent Blanc, Dario Simic, Javier Zanetti, Javier Farinos (Benoit Cauet 35), Luigi Di Biagio (Clarence Seedorf 46), Stéphane Dalmat, Vratislav Gresko; Christian Vieri, Alvaro Recoba.Manager: Marco Tardelli.

AC Milan: Sebastiano Rossi, Thomas Helveg, Alessandro Costacurta, Roque Junior, Paolo Maldini, Gennaro Gattuso, Federico Giunti (Andrés Guglielminpietro 71), Kakha Kaladze, Serginho, Andriy Shevchenko (Leonardo 82), Gianni Comandini (José Mari 58).Manager: Cesare Maldini

Major results in the Derby della Madonnina		
Milan 0 Inter 5	Serie A	1910
Inter 5 Milan 1	Serie A	1910
Milan 6 Inter 3	Serie A	1911
Inter 5 Milan 2	Serie A	1914
Milan 1 Inter 4	Serie A	1931
Inter 5 Milan 2	Serie A	1965
Inter 4 Milan 0	Serie A	1967
Milan 1 Inter 5	Serie A	1974
Milan 5 Inter 0	Coppa Italia	1998
Inter 0 Milan 6	Serie A	2001
Milan 0 Inter 4	Serie A	2009

CHAMPIONS LEAGUE FINAL, MAY 2008

Manchester United 1 Chelsea 1 (United won 6-4 on penalties)

Moscow's Luzhniki Stadium was the setting for the first European Cup Final between two English sides—and Chelsea's first appearance in the competition's last stage. It was 40 years since United had won their first European Cup and half a century since the side had been decimated by the Munich air disaster. It was also Premier League champions United versus runners-up Chelsea. Both teams had won their home league games against each other that term.

To add even more spice, Chelsea had won the previous year's FA Cup Final clash between the two sides and the Red Devils were victorious in the previous August's Community Shield clash between the two.

United took the lead after 26 minutes when Portugal winger Ronaldo headed home a cross from defender Brown. Chelsea keeper Cech was outstanding as the Red Devils looked to extend their lead, but in the dying stages of the first half a long-range shot from midfielder Essien deflected off defender Vidic and then Ferdinand, before Lampard pounced to stab home the equaliser.

Chelsea pushed for a winner for most of the second half, although Chelsea captain Terry cleared a shot from Giggs for United.

Extra time produced some dramatic action from both sides but it was Chelsea striker Drogba who created the headlines when he became only the second player to be sent off in a Champions League Final after he slapped Vidic with just four minutes of extra time to go. The game went to a penalty shootout that saw Argentina striker Tevez send Cech the wrong way and then Germany midfielder Ballack smash home for Chelsea. United's Carrick then scored and substitute Belletti made it 2-2 with his first kick of the game.

Ronaldo tried to fool the keeper with a stuttering run and failed to score. Lampard put Chelsea ahead before Hargreaves fired into the top corner. Defender Cole saw his shot touched by United's Dutch keeper van der Sar but still go into the net. Nani then scored, which meant Terry could win the cup for his side by scoring. But the defender slipped as he shot, the ball hit the post and went wide.

It then became sudden-death penalties and Anderson scored first for United, followed by Kalou sending the keeper the wrong way to make it 5-5. Veteran Giggs, making a record 759th appearance for United, kept his side in the game. But then France striker Anelka saw his spot-kick saved by Man of the Match van der Sar and United collected their third European Cup in front of a 69,500 crowd.

TEAMS

Manchester United: Edwin van der Sar, Wes Brown (Anderson 120+5), Rio Ferdinand, Nemanja Vidic, Patrice Evra, Owen Hargreaves, Paul Scholes (Giggs 87), Michael Carrick, Cristiano Ronaldo, Wayne Rooney (Nani 101), Carlos Tevez. Unused subs: Tomasz Kuszczak, John O'Shea, Mikael Silvestre, Darren Fletcher. Manager: Sir Alex Ferguson.

Chelsea: Petr Cech, Michael Essien, Ricardo Carvalho, John Terry, Ashley Cole, Claude Makelele (Juliano Belletti 120+4), Michael Ballack, Frank Lampard, Joe Cole (Nicolas Anelka 99), Florent Malouda (Salomon Kalou 92), Didier Drogba. Unused subs: Carlo Cudicini, Alex, John Obi Mikel, Andriy Shevchenko. Manager: Avram Grant

AFTER THE FINAL WHISTLE...

'It is a fantastic achievement. That is the first shootout I've won in a big game. I thought we were fantastic in the first half and should have been three or four up and they got a lucky break right on halftime.' Sir Alex Ferguson, Man United manager

'I thought we were going to lose. I had played well and scored but I had missed my penalty and it felt like the worst day of my life. But the lads did a proper job and I feel very proud for them. It means everything to me. Now it is the happiest day of my life.' **Cristiano Ronaldo, Man United midfielder**

'Terry was great all season, in the semi-final and this game. He is the reason they didn't create any chances. I feel sorry for him and the team. What can I say? Except in the beginning we dominated the game, we hit the post two times and then we lost on penalties. The team played excellently and I am very proud.' **Avram Grant, Chelsea manager**

'John was not in the first five to take a kick but things change during a game. It is unbelievable this should happen to him. We practised penalties so much and he was very confident. We were all very confident.' **Henk ten Cate, Chelsea assistant manager**

FA CUP FINAL, MAY 1953

Blackpool 4 Bolton Wanderers 3

This game is known as 'the Matthews Final', but in reality it was Stan Mortensen who created his own piece of football history. Blackpool's Stanley Matthews was the star of the show even though Mortensen recorded a hat trick, the only one scored at Wembley in the final of this trophy.

The Tangerines would make it third time lucky, having lost the finals of 1948 and

1951. But things didn't look good for them when Lofthouse, the Footballer of the Year, fired home after just 75 seconds to maintain his record of scoring in every round that season. Mortensen equalised after 35 minutesbut Bolton were back in front five minutes before the break when Langton lobbed the keeper.

Wanderers extended their lead to 3-1 on 55 through Bell, who played on despite injury as no substitutes were allowed in those days. Matthews then provided the inspiration for the fight-back. He provided a cross on 68 that gave Mortensen his second goal and with less than two minutes of the game left the player completed his hat trick from a free kick.

With seconds remaining, Matthews, then aged 38, provided another cross, this time for Perry to hit the winner in front of a 100,000 crowd. Matthews kept on playing in England's top-flight until the age of 50 and was still kicking a ball competitively at the age of 70. Knighted in 1965, the only footballer to be given the award while still playing, Sir Stanley died in 2000, aged 85.

TEAMS

Blackpool: George Farm, Eddie Shimwell, Tommy Garrett, Ewan Fenton, Harry Johnston, Cyril Robinson, Stanley Matthews, Ernie Taylor, Stan Mortensen, Jackie Mudie, Bill Perry. Manager: Joe Smith

Bolton Wanderers: Stan Hanson, John Ball, Ralph Banks, Johnny Wheeler, Malcolm Barrass, Eric Bell, Doug Holden, Willie Moir, Nat Lofthouse, Harold Hassall, Bobby Langton. Manager: Bill Ridding.

AFTER THE FINAL WHISTLE...

'We didn't click well in the first half and it wasn't going according to plan. We felt like coming off at 3-1. But something seemed to switch on and Blackpool started to play. The confidence seemed to be coming back.' **Cyril Robinson, Blackpool midfielder**

'I am told by one or two people that I was the match-winner. As a matter of fact I don't believe that, for the simple reason that we have here 11 match-winners.' **Sir Stanley Matthews, Blackpool winger**

WORLD CUP FINAL, JULY 1966

England 4 West Germany 2

This was the finest moment in English football, which included the only hat trick in a World Cup Final, a hotly disputed goal and one of the most famous statements in broadcasting. The hero of the moment, Geoff Hurst, might not even have played had goal-scoring legend Jimmy Greaves not been injured in the final group game.

Wembley Stadium was the setting for the 1966 Final in front of 94,000 fans, but the home support was stunned after just 12 minutes when Haller stabbed home after latching onto a miss-headed clearance. Just six minutes later Hurst headed the equaliser from a free kick taken by captain Moore. With just 13 minutes of the game remaining it looked like Peters had sealed a home victory when he put the Three Lions ahead, slotting home from close range after picking up a ball deflected by Hurst following a corner from Ball.

The Germans battled for an equaliser and with just seconds remaining were awarded a disputed free kick on the edge of the penalty area when Jack Charlton was judged to have fouled Seeler.

Emmerich hit the kick against the England wall but Weber seized on the rebound to hit the equaliser and take the game to extra time. England protests that Schnellinger had handled were brushed away. Eleven minutes into the first period of extra time Ball ran onto a pass from Stiles and crossed for Hurst who swivelled and shot. His effort hit the underside of the bar.

One of football's greatest debates then began over whether the ball had or had not crossed the goal line when it bounced on the ground. Referee Gottfried Dienst consulted with linesman Tofik Bakhramov and then awarded the goal. Replays in later years suggested the whole of the ball did not cross the line. A long ball from Moore saw Hurst complete his hat trick with virtually the last kick of the game as fans started to spill onto the pitch.

BBC TV commentator Kenneth Wolstenholme then uttered the famous words:'And here comes Hurst. He's got... some people are on the pitch, they think it's all over. It is now!' as the ball hit the back of the net to complete the scoring. For manager Ramsey, knighted in 1967, the outcome was a prediction come true. When he had taken over as boss of the national side in 1963 he had said England would win the 1966 World Cup. Ramsey was sacked when the Three Lions failed to reach the finals of the 1974 World Cup. He died in 1999 at the age of 79.

TEAMS

England: Gordon Banks, George Cohen, Jack Charlton, Bobby Moore, Ray Wilson, Nobby Stiles, Bobby Charlton, Alan Ball, Martin Peters, Roger Hunt, Geoff Hurst. Manager: Sir Alf Ramsey.

West Germany: Hans Tilkowski, Horst-Dieter Hottges, Willi Schulz, Wolfgang Weber, Karl-Heinz Schnellinger, Franz Beckenbauer, Wolfgang Overath, Helmut Haller, Uwe

Seeler, Sigfried Held, Lothar Emmerich. Manager: Helmut Schon

AFTER THE FINAL WHISTLE...

'The final was a long hard slog against a very good team. The pitch was very spongy, which made you move a yard or so slower. As we were preparing for extra time, Sir Alf said to us that the Germans were finished. We emerged as the stronger side but to be fair, German manager Helmut Schon was very gracious at the end and congratulated us, saying we were worthy winners.' **George Cohen, England defender**

'Franz Beckenbauer said we were the best team not only on the day but in the tournament. We had a great side and, even if one goal didn't count, we were still the strongest team in extra time. You don't win a World Cup by being lucky and we were the best team.' **Sir Geoff Hurst, England striker**

'It got off to a good start, and I think it ended well too, because we did well in getting to the final at Wembley and taking it into extra time. Finishing runner-up is not too bad for a young player.'

Franz Beckenbaur, West German midfielder, aged 20 when playing in the final

'It was not a goal. I'm absolutely certain. The ball was not behind the line. But that doesn't matter anymore.' **Uwe Seeler, West Germany captain**

PREMIER LEAGUE, SEPTEMBER 2009

Manchester United 4 Manchester City 3

With just five games of the season gone, the two Manchester sides went into their derby clash on the same number of points. And in what turned out to be a classic showdown the final seconds of the game produced an amazing conclusion. At first it looked as if a last-minute goal from Bellamy had snatched a point for City. But in a controversial amount of time added on for injuries substitute Owen grabbed a dramatic winner for United.

England striker Rooney got United off to a flyer with a close-range effort following a cross from full back Evra. But 14 minutes later the visitors were level. Former United striker Tevez sent the ball through to Barry who scored from 18 yards. United's good play faded but the two sides went in level at the break.

Just four minutes after the re-start Wales winger Giggs crossed and Scotland midfielder Fletcher headed home at the far post to make it 2-1 to United. But the Red Devils were ahead for less than three minutes as Wales striker Bellamy lashed home an amazing left wing effort from 25 yards.

City's Republic of Ireland keeper Given was forced into a string of heroic saves before Bulgaria striker Berbatov was replaced by former England frontman Owen.

With ten minutes left on the clock United finally regained the lead, Fletcher made it 3-2 when he headed home a Giggs' free kick. United looked to have the points in the bag until a last-minute slip by defender Ferdinand who gave away the ball to Bulgaria midfielder Petrov, who then put Bellamy through for his second goal and the equaliser.

Referee Martin Atkinson added four minutes of injury time but it was in the 96th—two minutes after the game should have finished—that Owen picked up a ball from Giggs and finished in his typical clinical style to give United the spoils.

TEAMS

Manchester United: Ben Foster, Patrice Evra, Rio Ferdinand, Nemanja Vidic, John O'Shea, Anderson (Michael Carrick 90), Ryan Giggs, Park Ji-sung (Antonio Valencia 62), Darren Fletcher, Dimitar Berbatov (Michael Owen 78), Wayne Rooney. Unused subs: Tomasz Kuszczak, Gary Neville, Jonny Evans, Nani. Manager: Sir Alex Ferguson.

Manchester City: Shay Given, Micah Richards, Wayne Bridge, Joleon Lescott, Kolo Toure, Stephen Ireland, Shaun Wright-Phillips, Gareth Barry, Nigel De Jong (Martin Petrov 83), Carlos Tevez, Craig Bellamy. Unused subs: Stuart Taylor, Pablo Zabaleta, Javier Garrido, Sylvinho, Vladimir Weiss, Michael Ball. Manager: Mark Hughes

AFTER THE FINAL WHISTLE...

'The mistakes probably made it the best derby of all time. What would you rather have, a 6-0 win or the greatest derby of all time? I would prefer to win 6-0. Michael [Owen] was only on for something like 17 minutes. He was the best man to be on there when the game is going to be in their penalty box. There is no one better at taking chances.' **Sir Alex Ferguson, Manchester United manager**

'We need an explanation because I don't know why the referee has added that amount of time on. Obviously, he has played too much time and we ended up playing 97 minutes. United were given a little more time than they should have been given to get the goal.' **Mark Hughes, Manchester City manager**

PREMIER LEAGUE, MAY 2012

Manchester City 3 Queens Park Rangers 2

It was the final day of the 2011–12 season and the two Manchester sides kicked off their games locked on the same number of points. Little did the players and fans of both United and City know of the drama that was going to unfold during the next 90 minutes.

The script could not have been written any better for a big film drama as City looked to land their first top tier title for 44 years…and at the expense of their most bitter rivals. City knew they had to beat relegation-threatened QPR at the Etihad Stadium if their neighbours United won at Sunderland.

And things got off to a bad start for City when news filtered back to Manchester that United had taken the lead at Sunderland with a 20th minute strike from England forward Rooney. But with six minutes to go to the break defender Zabaleta put City ahead thanks to a ball from Toure. If the scores stayed as they were, City would be champions on goal difference.

But the hearts of the home-side fans, already deflated by the loss to injury of Toure shortly before the break, looked like they could be broken when Cisse took advantage of a poor clearance to hit an equaliser for QPR just three minutes into the second half. They were given hope when Rangers midfielder Barton was shown a red card for raising his arm to Argentina striker Tevez. Surely City, with their extra man, could now push on to get the result they needed?

It didn't work out quite like that…as Mackie headed ten-man QPR ahead on 66 minutes. Now it was United, still winning at Sunderland, who would win the league.

As the clock ticked down it appeared that City had blown the chance of their first Premier League title. Some fans were in tears and others left the ground early. Those who stayed to the end saw one of the most remarkable turnarounds ever and certainly the most amazing end to a top-flight season.

With two minutes of injury time already played Dzeko headed an equaliser. A draw would still not be enough for City's title hopes. The game at Sunderland had finished and United had won 1-0. As the referee looked at his watch to check how many seconds of the five minutes of injury time were left at the Etihad, Argentina striker Aguero powered into the penalty area and smashed home the winner, his 30th goal of the season.

From being eight points behind United with five weeks of the season left, City had done the unthinkable and pulled level with their neighbours. And City's superior goal difference meant they had won the Premier League title in front of a 48,000 crowd of mostly home supporters.

Both sides finished with 89 points—United's best total for a 38-game season—but City's goal difference was 64 to United's 56. Despite defeat QPR beat their own relegation fears thanks to results elsewhere going in their favour.

TEAMS

Manchester City: Joe Hart, Vincent Kompany, Pablo Zabaleta, Joleon Lescott, Gael Clichy, Gary Barry (Edin Dzeko 69), Samir Nasri, David Silva, Yaya Toure (Nigel de Jong 44), Sergio Aguero, Carlos Tevez (Mario Balotelli 75). Unused subs: Costel Pantilimon, Micah Richards, Aleksandar Kolarov, James Milner. Manager: Roberto Mancini

QPR: Paddy Kenny, Clint Hill, Taye Taiwo, Anton Ferdinand, Nedum Onuoha, Shaun Derry, Joey Barton, Shaun Wright-Phillips, Jamie Mackie, Djibril Cisse (Traore 59), Bobby Zamora (Jay Bothroyd 76). Unused subs: Radek Cerny, Danny Gabbidon, Adel Taarabt, Akos Buzsaky, DJ Campbell. Manager: Mark Hughes

AFTER THE FINAL WHISTLE...

'To win like this, I think it will be impossible for the next 100 years. It's probably the best moment for me. When I saw the time, 89 minutes, I thought it was finished.' **Roberto Mancini, Man City manager**

'If we had pulled it off and won the game, it would have been the greatest Premier League performance in history given the significance of the game and the attention focused on it. The one criticism is that we understood we were safe just prior to their winning goal. Maybe we just switched off. I have never been involved in anything like that but Roberto would have to admit he has been lucky.' **Mark Hughes, QPR manager**

FA CUP FINAL, APRIL 1923

Bolton Wanderers 2 West Ham United 0

The first football match at the original Wembley Stadium is remembered more as the 'White Horse Final' rather than for the actual result! Wembley was not due to be opened until the following year but building work was completed ahead of schedule. An official attendance of 126,000 was scorned by unofficial estimates that 300,000 had crammed into the London ground.

In the build-up to the game more police and barriers were brought in to control the excessive crowds and the extra security included PC George Scorey on his horse Billy. Black and white news footage showed the grey horse as being white—and although other mounted police were there on the day, it is the image of Billy and his rider that got the Final its name because the pair were the dominant image on cinema newsreels. Horse and rider became so famous that the Whitehorse Bridge became part of the new Wembley Stadium when it opened in 2007.

The mass crowds meant the game kicked off 45 minutes late but it took less than two minutes for Jack to put Bolton ahead—his shot so hard that a fan behind the goal was knocked out cold by the power of the ball. Sheer pressure from the number of fans in the crowd resulted in fans spilling onto the pitch and play was halted for a time.

Bolton kept pressing but it wasn't until eight minutes into the second half—when West Ham had become more of a force—that Wanderers increased their lead. Vizard played the ball to Jack Smith who fired home, but Hammers' players claimed the ball had hit the goalpost before bouncing back into play. The referee allowed the goal, which prompted a mass exit of fans as many of them were from East London and had been supporting West Ham.

TEAMS

Bolton Wanderers: Dick Pym, Bob Haworth, Alex Finney, Harry Nuttall, Jimmy Seddon, Billy Jennings, Billy Butler, David Jack, Jack Smith, Joe Smith, Ted Vizard. Manager: Charles Foweraker

West Ham United: Ted Hufton, Billy Henderson, Jack Young, Syd Bishop, George Kay, Jack Tresadern, Dick Richards, Billy Brown, Vic Watson, Billy Moore, Jimmy Ruffell. Manager: Syd King

AFTER THE FINAL WHISTLE...

'It was that white horse thumping its feet into the pitch that made it hopeless. Our wingers were tumbling all over the place, tripping up in great ruts and holes.' **Charlie Paynter, West Ham trainer**

EL CLASICO

Real Madrid v Barcelona

El Clasico is the game that features Spanish rivals Real Madrid taking on Barcelona. The two giants are guaranteed two El Clasico meetings every season when they clash in La Liga.

It is believed to be the most watched match in the world, beamed by television to millions of fans around the world.

An amazing 500 million followers of the beautiful game are reported to have watched the two-legged Champions League semi-final meeting between the two sides in 2005, which Madrid edged 3-1. Of the 260 meetings between the two sides until the end of the season 2013–14, Barca had won 107 games and had 58 draws.

Madrid have won 70 of La Liga clashes between the sides, compared to Barca's 66 victories.

Let's presume that most teams don't really put much emphasis on friendly results. That would give Real Madrid a lucky escape, as the biggest thrashing in this fixture was the 13-0 win by Barcelona in March 1982…

Barca got their own let off from the 11-1 hiding they took at the hands of Madrid in June 1943. There were allegations of match fixing and threats in that Copa del Rey semi-final clash and the Spanish FA outlawed the result. Madrid went on to get beaten in the final! The top scorer in this hotly contested game is Argentina striker Lionel Messi with 21 league and cup goals for Barca… so far! With many years of his career still to play and no sign that he wants to leave Barcelona he's likely to add a few more goals to that total! His fellow countryman, Alfredo Di Stéfano—who played for Madrid from 1953–64—hit 18 goals in the El Clasico to be Real's top scorer in the fixture.

Major El Clasico Results	
Real Madrid 8 Barcelona 2	February 1935
Barcelona 5 Real Madrid 0	April 1935
Barcelona 5 Real Madrid 0	March 1945
Real Madrid 6 Barcelona 1	September 1949
Barcelona 7 Real Madrid 2	September 1950
Real Madrid 5 Barcelona 0	October 1953
Real Madrid 0 Barcelona 5	February 1974
Barcelona 5 Madrid 0	January 1994
Real Madrid 5 Barcelona 0	January 1995
Barcelona 5 Real Madrid 0	November 2010

AFTER THE FINAL WHISTLE...

'I won my four Clasicos as a coach? No, we won them.' **Pep Guardiola, former Barca boss**

'All players like playing in games like this, but there's also a lot of tension and lots of intensity in the games. There are factors that lead you to where games turn out one way or the other.' **Andrés Iniesta, Barcelona midfielder**

'It's such a special occasion. Historically it's one of the best derbies in the world, if not the best.' **David Beckham, former Real Madrid midfielder**

'El Clasico is important, not only for the race to the title, but for the general mood of the team. It is a game that is different to any other game.' **Carlo Ancelotti, Real Madrid manager**

OLD FIRM DERBY, JANUARY 1943

Rangers 8 Celtic 1

The Scots just love to celebrate New Year. But on 1 January 1943 just one half of

Glasgow was celebrating. Rangers' supporters couldn't have got a better start to the year than the record 8-1 victory over their city rivals Celtic. The result came in the unofficial wartime Scottish Southern League and saw Gillick rattle in a hat trick.

Rangers were 2-1 up at halftime. Duncanson scored in the first minute from close range and Waddle added to the lead with a screamer after just five minutes. Duncan pulled a goal back before the end of ten minutes. Gillick scored the third just after halftime and then Young a spectacular fourth from the halfway line.

Celtic launched a strong verbal attack on the referee, claiming a player was offside when Young scored. The protests led to Celtic full back McDonald being sent off. His side were down to nine men just five minutes later when right half Lynch was also shown a red card. They were fined £10 and £5 respectively and also received bans.

Waddell got the fifth on 70 minutes, then Young added a penalty after Dornan had fisted away a header from Gillick. Gillick got his second five minutes from time and completed his hat trick as he hit Rangers' eighth. Defeat for the Bhoys meant they had lost seven Old Firm derbies in a row. Just 30,000 were at Ibrox to see the latest home win.

The result was never officially recognised as both sides had players away fighting in World War II; this was a time when many teams had 'guests' boosting their squads. *The Glasgow Herald* has referred to the game as being a record score line between the two sides, and Rangers have also suggested it should have that status.

Although there have been a number of Old Firm clashes with a four-goal difference between the two sides, only one other result came close to the 1943 outcome—when Celtic beat Rangers 7-1 in the Scottish League Cup in October 1957. Boss of Rangers that day was Scott Symon, who had been a player when the 'Gers inflicted the 8-1 defeat on the Bhoys in 1943.

TEAMS

Rangers: Jerry Dawson, Dougie Gray, Jock Shaw, Adam Little, George Young, Scot Symon, Willie Waddell, Alex Venters, Torry Gillick, Charlie Johnston, Jimmy Duncanson. Manager: Bill Struth

Celtic: Willie Miller, Malky McDonald, Henry Dornan, Matt Lynch, Willie Corbett, George Paterson, Jimmy Delaney, Pat Mcauley, Seton Airlie, James McGowan, Davey Duncan. Manager: Jimmy McStay

Major Results in the Old Firm Derby	
Rangers 5 Celtic 0, January, 1894	Division One
Celtic 6 Rangers 2, January 1896	Division One
Celtic 4 Rangers 0, January, 1898	Division One
Rangers 4 Celtic 0, January, 1899	Division One
Celtic 4 Rangers 0, March, 1900	Scottish Cup
Celtic 4 Rangers 0, January, 1914	Division One
Celtic 5 Rangers 0, March, 1925	Scottish Cup
Rangers 4 Celtic 0, April, 1928	Scottish Cup
Celtic 6 Rangers 2, January, 1939	Division One
Celtic 5 Rangers 1, January, 1966	Division One
Celtic 4 Rangers 0, April, 1969	Scottish Cup Final
Rangers 5 Celtic 1, August, 1988	Scottish Premier Division
Celtic 5 Rangers 1, November, 1998	Scottish Premier League
Celtic 6 Rangers 2, August, 2000	Scottish Premier League
Rangers 5 Celtic 1, November, 2000	Scottish Premier League

PREMIER LEAGUE, MARCH 1995

Manchester United 9 Ipswich Town 0

This was the Premier League's biggest victory and a game that carved out a place in history for Manchester United striker Andy Cole. The England hit man became the first player to score five goals in the Premier League as the Red Devils recorded their biggest win in 103 years. There were almost 48,000 spectators inside Old Trafford to see the home side gain revenge for a 3-2 defeat against Ipswich at Portman Road earlier in the season.

Republic of Ireland midfielder Keane began the rout in the 15th minute with a shot from outside the area, and four minutes later Cole hit the first of his five, thanks to a pass from Giggs. Cole then latched onto a rebound on 37 to make it 3-0 at halftime. The second period was just eight minutes old when Cole completed his hat trick by heading home an Irwin cross.

Two minutes later Wales forward Hughes made it 5-0, once again thanks to a Giggs assist. Just four minutes after his first strike Hughes added a second, this time a header after Ipswich keeper Forest had blocked an attempt from Giggs. Cole, who had only recently joined United for £6 million from Newcastle United, added his fourth on 65, a left-foot volley.

England midfielder Ince took the score to 8-0 on 72. The Ipswich keeper handled outside of the box and Ince took the free kick quickly to catch the shot-stopper off-guard. But it was Cole's day and he completed his record total and a new scoring best for the Red Devils when he hit his fifth goal just three minutes from time. This time it was a close-range effort following a ball headed down from defender Pallister.

The win meant United kept up the pressure on Blackburn Rovers at the top of the table but at the end of the campaign they were pipped for the title by a point. Ipswich were relegated in bottom position.

TEAMS

Manchester United: Peter Schmeichel, Roy Keane (Lee Sharpe 46), Steve Bruce (Nicky Butt 79), Gary Pallister, Denis Irwin, Andriy Kanchelskis, Brian McClair, Paul Ince, Ryan Giggs, Andy Cole, Mark Hughes. Unused sub: Gary Walsh. Manager: Sir Alex Ferguson

Ipswich Town: Craig Forrest, Frank Yallop, John Wark, David Linighan, Neil Thompson, Steve Palmer, Geraint Williams, Steve Sedgley, Stuart Slater, Lee Chapman (Ian Marshall 63), Alex Mathie. Unused subs: Phil Morgan, Paul Mason. Manager: George Burley

AFTER THE FINAL WHISTLE…

'We were going through a rebuilding process at Ipswich under a new manager in George Burley and Manchester United were untouchable. It was 8-0 with 25 minutes to go and I saw Sir Alex telling his players to calm down. I don't think he wanted to humiliate us anymore. We actually had a shot at goal in the first 10 minutes but it was one-way traffic after that and I remember Ian Marshall hiding behind a goalpost because he did not want to go on!' **Alex Mathie, Ipswich striker**

WORLD CUP FINAL, JUNE 1970

Brazil 4 Italy 1

The 108,000 crowd inside Mexico City's Estadio Azteca witnessed a football masterclass as two World Cup-winners faced each other in the final for the first time. And it was no surprise that the skills of Pelé shone in a game that had football purists drooling.

Pelé got favourites Brazil off to a flying start with a fantastic header after 18 minutes—although Italy equalised eight minutes before halftime when Boninsegna picked up a ball than had been back-heeled by Clodoaldo. Some 66 minutes of the game had gone when Gerson unleashed a left-footed shot that put Brazil back in front.

Then Pelé, appearing in his last World Cup Final, laid off the ball for Jairzinho—who had scored in every round—to make it 3-1 after 71 minutes. And with just three minutes remaining Pelé was once again the creator, this time giving captain Alberto the chance to hammer in the Brazilians' fourth—a goal still rated as one of the best ever in a World Cup Final.

Brazil, winners in 1958 and 1962, were allowed to keep the trophy after this third victory. But when the team returned home the cup was stolen and never seen again.

TEAMS

Brazil: Felix, Carlos Alberto, Brito, Piazza, Everaldo, Clodoaldo, Gerson, Rivelino, Jairzinho, Tostao, Pelé. Manager: Mario Zagallo

Italy: Enrico Albertosi, Tarcisio Burgnich, Pierluigi Cera, Roberto Rosato, Giacinto Facchetti, Mario Bertini (Antonio Juliano 75), Sandro Mazzola, Giancarlo De Sisti, Angelo Domenghini, Roberto Boninsegna (Gianni Rivera 84), Luigi Riva. Manager: Ferruccio Valcareggi

AFTER THE FINAL WHISTLE...

'After the third goal by Jairzinho I knew we had won, and I began to cry with joy. I played the last fifteen minutes with tears in my eyes.' **Tostao, Brazil forward**

'I told myself before the game that Pelé was made of skin and bone like everyone else. Later I realised I was wrong.' **Tarcisio Burgnich, Italy defender**

'We felt very good before the tournament. Pelé was saying that we were going to win, and if Pelé was saying that, then we were going to win the World Cup.' **Carlos Alberto, Brazil captain**

WORLD CUP QUALIFIER 2002, SEPTEMBER 2001

Germany 1 England 5

It was Mission Impossible. England had to win in Germany. The Three Lions had to defeat the home side to keep alive their hopes of automatic qualification to the finals of World Cup 2002.

But the side managed by Sven-Goran Eriksson knew they would face a German team that had only lost once in 60 World Cup qualifiers.

This was a team that had already beaten England 1-0 the previous year in the final game at the old Wembley Stadium, before it was demolished. England had just one victory against the Germans since their 1966 World Cup win and their hosts were unbeaten on home soil since 1973.

When England fell behind after just six minutes to a goal from Carsten Jancker it looked like their dream of qualification could become a nightmare. But what then unfolded in front of 63,000 fans at Munich's Olympic Stadium sent shockwaves through world football.

England equalised on 13 minutes through Owen and the team went on to record a stunning 5-1 victory with the young Liverpool striker completing a hat trick. Owen's first goal came after the player was fouled on the edge of the opposition penalty area. Captain Beckham's free kick was headed into the area by Neville, where Barmby headed down to Owen who volleyed the ball into the net.

It looked like the score would remain 1-1 at the break but in injury time England won another free kick, once again taken by Beckham. The ball was crossed to Ferdinand who headed it to Gerrard who unleashed a shot into the corner of the next. It was Gerrard's first goal for his country.

The second half was just three minutes old when Beckham put a ball over to Heskey to head down to the unmarked Owen to get his second of the game. The Germans were still not out of the game, but after 66 minutes Gerrard won the ball and slipped in through to his club teammate Owen, who raced into the box to complete his hat trick and make it 4-1 to England. It meant the Liverpool forward had become the first England player since the 1966 World Cup Final to score a hat trick against Germany.

England were put under pressure but with 16 minutes remaining defender Ferdinand won the ball and sent it up pitch to midfielder Scholes who worked with Beckham to put Heskey through.

The burly striker completed the scoring—the third Liverpool player to notch in the game! Owen, who still regards this as one of the biggest highlights of his career, went through the usual process of exchanging shirts with the opposition, then realised that the England shirt on this occasion was something he really wanted to keep.

'I had to go and get it back because I wanted to frame it', he admitted. England finished the qualifying campaign top of their group and gained automatic entry to the World Cup Finals in Japan and Korea. The Germans beat Ukraine in a play-off to get their place. England were eliminated 2-1 by Brazil at the quarter-final stage in the Far East. Germany were beaten 2-0 in the final by Brazil.

TEAMS

Germany: Oliver Kahn, Christian Worns (Gerald Asamoah 45), Jorg Bohme, Thomas Linke, Jens Nowotny, Dietmar Hamann, Marko Rehmer, Michael Ballack (Miroslav Klose 65), Carsten Jancker, Sebastian Deisler, Oliver Neuville (Sebastian Kehl 78). Unused subs: Jens Lehmann, Oliver Bierhoff, Frank Baumann, Christian Ziege. Manager: Rudi Voller

England: David Seaman, Gary Neville, Ashley Cole, Steven Gerrard (Owen Hargreaves 78), Rio Ferdinand, Sol Campbell, David Beckham, Paul Scholes (Jamie Carragher 83), Emile Heskey, Michael Owen, Nick Barmby (Steve McManaman 64). Unused subs: Nigel Martyn, Gareth Southgate, Andy Cole, Robbie Fowler. Manager: Sven-Goran Eriksson

AFTER THE FINAL WHISTLE...

'I was so frustrated being 1-0 down. Then, all of a sudden, we started playing. You could see the confidence growing through the team. I think about that game almost every day. It was such an important game for us to win and the team performance was exceptional.' **David Beckham, England midfielder**

'To score my first goal for England in a game of that magnitude against our biggest rivals was a dream come true. I'd been in the squad for less than 18 months. I was only a baby in terms of international football.' **Steven Gerrard, England midfielder**

'I always said and always believed we could beat Germany, but I couldn't believe 5-1. It was too much—the difference between the teams was maybe not so great, but we played very, very well.' **Sven Goran Eriksson, England manager**

'It was disappointing for us but losing wasn't the end of the world. The squad came together after the game, we got through our play-off against Ukraine and we actually made it to the World Cup Final. In hindsight, it wasn't a bad game to lose.' **Dietmar Hamann, Germany midfielder**

INTERNATIONAL FRIENDLY, NOVEMBER 1953

England 3 Hungary 6

Despite being Olympic champions and having gone three years without defeat, Hungary were underestimated by England when they arrived at Wembley for this friendly. Hungary had gone 24 games without defeat and were ranked No.1 in the world. But England, unbeaten at home by overseas opposition—except one loss to the Republic of Ireland four years earlier—were confused by their visitors' 4-2-4 formation and the fact that some of the team did not wear shirt numbers that corresponded to the positions they played—sides those days wore the numbers one to nine.

Hidegkuti gave the Three Lions a rude awakening with the opening goal after just 90 seconds.

Sewell equalised with 13 minutes gone but the Hungarians then added three more goals before the break: Hidegkuti netting his second on 20 and Puskas scoring on 24 and 27. Mortensen managed to pull one back seven minutes before halftime to make it 2-4 at the break.

Just five minutes into the second half Bozsik gave the visitors their fifth goal and three minutes later Hidegkuti completed his hat trick.

Ramsey completed the scoring in the 57th minute from the penalty spot after Grosics had fouled Robb. Observers recorded 35 Hungarian shots on goal to England's five in what was to be known as 'The match of the century.' Eckersley, Ramsey, Robb, Johnston, Mortensen and Taylor did not represent their country again and the result led to a complete re-think about the game in England. Yet just six months later England were hammered 7-1 by Hungary in Budapest.

TEAMS

England: Gil Merrick, Alf Ramsey, Bill Eckersley, Billy Wright, Harry Johnson, Jimmy Dickinson, Stanley Matthews, Ernie Taylor, Stan Mortensen, Jackie Sewell, George Robb. Manager: Walter Winterbottom

Hungary: Gyula Grosics (Sandor Géller 78), Gyula Lorant, Jeno Buzanszky, Jozsef Zakarias, Mihaly Lantos, Jozsef Bozsik, Nandor Hidegkuti, Laszlo Budai, Sandor Kocsis, Ferenc Puskas, Zoltan Czibor. Manager: Gusztav Sebes

AFTER THE FINAL WHISTLE…

'We completely underestimated the advances that Hungary had made and not only tactically.' **Billy Wright, England captain**

'When we attacked, everyone attacked, and in defence it was the same. We were the prototype for Total Football.' **Ferenc Puskas, Hungary forward**

PREMIER LEAGUE, SEPTEMBER 1999

Newcastle 8 Sheffield Wednesday 0

Sir Bobby Robson's arrival as manager at his boyhood heroes Newcastle United did not get off to a good start: the side was beaten 1-0 at Chelsea by a controversial penalty. But the following weekend the Geordies celebrated Robson's first home game in charge with some style. The staggering 8-0 score line against Sheffield Wednesday gave the Magpies their first win of the season; their first league win since the previous April; their first home win since February; and a record five goals by legendary striker Alan Shearer. Robson's arrival at St. James' Park had raised fans' hopes of a return to the swashbuckling football they had enjoyed under Kevin Keegan, following a drab period when Ruud Gullit was boss.

Gullit had committed the cardinal sin of leaving local hero and goal-scoring machine Shearer plus midfield marvel Lee, out of the side for his last game in charge, the crucial home derby against Sunderland, which Newcastle lost. But even die-hard supporters could not have predicted what would happen in Robson's second game.

Northern Ireland defender Hughes was the unlikely first scorer with a header after just 11 minutes. Shearer then notched a hat trick in a 12-minute spell. First he flicked home a Solano cross; then he hit a penalty after Thome handled; and completed his three strikes just three minutes from halftime with a close range effort from a Dyer cross.

Dyer also got on the score sheet less than a minute after the re-start and then the crowd had to wait until 78 minutes for Speed to head home a Solano corner. Shearer got his fourth when he latched onto a loose ball on 81. With just six minutes remaining Robinson was brought down in the area and Shearer blasted home his second spot-kick.

Shearer became only the second player to hit five goals in one Premier League game. The first man to do so was Manchester United's Andy Cole, in 1995, another player who, like Shearer, had worn the famed No.9 shirt at Newcastle. At halftime Sir Bobby had told Shearer he would give him a Mars bar if he finished the game with five goals!

TEAMS

Newcastle: Steve Harper, Warren Barton, Aaron Hughes, Alain Goma, Didier Domi (Stephen Glass 81), Nobby Solano, Robert Lee, Gary Speed, Kieron Dyer (Paul Robinson 63), Temur Ketsbaia (Jamie McClen 78), Alan Shearer. Unused subs: Tommy Wright, David Beharall. Manager: Sir Bobby Robson

Sheffield Wednesday: Kevin Pressman, Ian Nolan, Emerson Thome, Des Walker, Jon Newsome, Petter Rudi (Steve Haslam 45), Danny Sonner, Simon Donnelly (Gerald Sibon 83), Niclas Alexandersson, Gilles De Bilde, Andy Booth (Benito Carbone 27). Unused subs: Pavel Srnicek, Phil O'Donnell. Manager: Danny Wilson

AFTER THE FINAL WHISTLE…

'Confidence was at an all-time low, including for myself. If he [Bobby Robson] hadn't come in I would probably have had to leave the football club. The first game that he was there, he took some of the senior players into his room and just speaking to us for half an hour he gave us confidence without actually seeing us play.' **Alan Shearer, Newcastle United striker**

'The players let us down and it's time we started facing up to it. I haven't told the players. The manager is the bloke who looks after the players. We have to all get stuck in and make it work.' **Dave Richards, Sheffield Wednesday chairman**

PREMIER LEAGUE, NOVEMBER 2009

Tottenham 9 Wigan 1

Records tumbled when Jermain Defoe hit five goals for Tottenham Hotspur in their 9-1 demolition of Wigan Athletic. The England striker recorded the second fastest hat trick in Premier League history, his three goals coming in just seven minutes—slightly longer than Robbie Fowler's best for Liverpool in 1994.

Defoe was also only the third player to score five goals in a Premier League fixture, following Andy Cole of Manchester United and Newcastle United's Alan Shearer, and the fourth Spurs player to score five goals, following Ted Harper (1930), Alf Stokes (1957) and Les Allen (1960).

Tottenham became the second team to hit nine goals in a Premier League fixture, following the Manchester United 9 Ipswich Town 0 result of 1995. This was also Tottenham's biggest victory since 1977 when they had beaten Bristol Rovers 9-0.

Fellow England striker Crouch headed Spurs to the lead from a Lennon cross after nine minutes before Defoe slotted home from close range just six minutes after the break. Lennon provided the crosses for Defoe's second on 54 and his hat trick on 58 to give him his second triple of the season.

Wigan's Austrian defender Scharner replied between those two Defoe goals, on 57 minutes.

Winger Lennon got in on the scoring act on 64 before Corluka and Kranjcar provided the balls for Defoe's fourth and fifth. Wigan, whose keeper Kirkland had pulled off a series of impressive saves, couldn't stop a Bentley free kick that hit the woodwork, bouncing in to the net off his body two minutes from time. And in time added on Kranjcar turned and smashed the ball into the net to complete the shot-stopper's misery.

TEAMS

Tottenham Hotspure: Heurelho Gomes, Michael Dawson, Vedran Corluka, Benoit Assou-Ekotto (Sébastien Bassong 81), Jonathan Woodgate, Tom Huddlestone, Aaron Lennon (David Bentley 79), Wilson Palacios (Jermaine Jenas 84), Niko Kranjcar,

Peter Crouch, Jermain Defoe. *Unused subs: Ben Alnwick, Alan Hutton, Roman Pavlyuchenko, Robbie Keane. Manager: Harry Redknapp*

Wigan: Chris Kirkland, Erik Edman, Paul Scharner, Emmerson Boyce, Titus Bramble, Mario Melchiot (Cho Won-hee 85), Hendry Thomas (Jordi Gomez 67), Charles N'Zogbia, Mohamed Diamé, Jason Scotland, Hugo Rodallega. Unused subs: Mike Pollitt, Maynor Figueroa, Jason Koumas, Scott Sinclair, Olivier Kapo. Manager: Roberto Martinez

AFTER THE FINAL WHISTLE…

'It was unacceptable and unexpected. The way we defended in key moments was not good enough. I am embarrassed as it's a result we don't want to be associated with. I've never been involved in a game like this.' **Roberto Martinez, Wigan manager**

'I had a funny feeling before the game. Adidas gave me a pair of green boots and I tried them on before the game but [striker coach] Clive Allen said I couldn't wear them, so I changed them… Even when I got the fifth [goal] I wanted another and another.' **Jermain Defoe, Tottenham striker**

'When he [Defoe] concentrates and plays his football, he can be unstoppable. He's an amazing finisher.' **Harry Redknapp, Tottenham Hotspurr manager**

FA CUP FIRST ROUND, NOVEMBER 1971

AFC Bournemouth 11 Margate 0

It was such an inconsequential FA Cup tie that the national media had all but overlooked this first round clash between Third Division Bournemouth and non-league Margate. But radio, television and national newspapers soon became interested in the final result when they heard that striker Ted MacDougall had scored a record nine goals for Bournemouth.

The hitman that Cherries' supporters had dubbed 'Supermac' and 'Super Ted' became an overnight media sensation—although he had scored six goals against Oxford in the same round the previous season! MacDougall scored five in the first half against Margate whose manager reportedly asked Bournemouth gaffer John Bond to take the striker off at halftime!

Some 12,000 fans were in the ground as Division Three leaders Bournemouth took on the Southern League part-timers, whose boss Riggs had only taken the job the previous week. MacDougall scored after just 90 seconds when he latched onto a bad pass back that was dropped by the keeper. Supermac's first hat trick of the game was complete in 25 minutes and he ran riot for the rest of the match, with many watchers claiming that every time he touched the ball it went into the net.

Machin and Cave scored the other Bournemouth goals. MacDougall went on to score a total of 47 goals that season, two less than he had the previous term! Super Ted's nine goals meant he had beaten the previous FA Cup best of seven goals by one scorer in one game, scored in 1922 by Billy Minter of St Albans. The Margate keeper claimed one of the goals was actually a bad pass back—but even if MacDougall had hit eight he would have set a new best.

MacDougall went on to play for Manchester United and West Ham before rejoining his former boss Bond, then at Norwich City, and on to Southampton before a return to Bournemouth.

TEAMS

Bournemouth: Fred Davies, Mel Machin, Bill Kitchener, John Benson, David Jones, Tony Powell, Micky Cave, Ted MacDougall, Phil Bowyer, Keith Miller, Tony Scott. Sub: Jim De Garis. Manager: John Bond

Margate: Chic Brodie, Dai Yorath, Alan Butterfield, Eddie Clayton, David Paton, Bob Wickens, David Jarman, John Wickens, Barry Brown, John Kearns, John Baber. Sub: Ray Summers. Manager: Les Rigg

AFTER THE FINAL WHISTLE…

'I was disappointed as I thought I should have got 11.' **Ted MacDougall, Bournemouth striker**

'It was chucking it down with rain and after five minutes the referee stopped the game and asked our keeper Chic Brodie to change his shorts. It affected the game because we were doing reasonably well until that point and then this lunatic made us do that.' **Les Rigg, Margate manager**

EUROPEAN CUP FINAL, MAY 1967

Celtic 2 Inter Milan 1

It wasn't quite David v Goliath, but the champions of Scotland against the top team in Italy did appear to be a mismatch. Celtic had won their 21st league title the previous season to qualify for the European Cup and at Lisbon's Estadio Nacional Stadium they made their first appearance in the final.

Inter Milan, Italy's League champions for the tenth time, had been European Cup winners in 1964 and 1965 and were favourites to win the trophy yet again. The solid defending of the Italians was favoured to hold off the attacking qualities of the Glasgow side. But Celtic were determined to be the first British team to win the European Cup, despite missing their leading scorer Joe McBride.

It didn't look good for the Bhoys when they went behind to a penalty after just seven minutes. Craig fouled Cappellini in the area and Mazzola converted the spot-kick. That was the signal for the Italians to shut up shop and play their usual defensive game. Celtic went on the attack and although they had some good efforts on goal they couldn't make a breakthrough.

Inter were under so much pressure they were unable to mount any serious attack on the Bhoys, but it appeared Celtic might struggle to score. Then, with 63 minutes gone, Murdoch and Craig got the ball into enough space for Gemmell to get in a shot that beat the Inter keeper. As the clock ticked down the game remained deadlocked until just over five minutes from the end. Murdoch then shot at goal and Chalmers turned the ball into the net.

Celtic fans among the 45,000 crowd invaded the pitch to celebrate victory and the presentation of the cup was delayed. Some players were left shirtless for the presentation as supporters from Scotland collected souvenirs. Amazingly, all of Celtic's players had been born within 30 miles of the side's home city. Their success in Portugal earned them the title of the 'Lisbon Lions' and a stand at the Celtic Park ground was later named after them.

Celtic's historic victory followed earlier successes that season when they had once again been crowned Scottish League champions and won both the Scottish FA and League Cups. Around 50,000 fans were at Celtic Park to welcome them home from the final and admire the European Cup.

European defeat for Inter capped a miserable end to their season. They had already lost their league title and fallen at the semi-final stages of both Italian domestic cups.

TEAMS

Celtic: Ronnie Simpson, Jim Craig, Billy McNeill, John Clark, Tommy Gemmell, Bobby Murdoch, Bertie Auld, Jimmy Johnstone, Willie Wallace, Stevie Chalmers, Bobby Lennox. Manager: Jock Stein.

Inter Milan: Giuliano Sarti, Armando Picchi, Tarcisio Burgnich, Aristide Guarneri, Giacinto Facchetti, Gianfranco Bedin, Mauro Bicicli, Mario Corso, Angelo Domenghini, Sandro Mazzola, Renato Cappellini. Manager: Helenio Herrera

AFTER THE FINAL WHISTLE...

'Winning the European Cup is one of the club's finest ever moments and obviously an achievement which all the players hold very dear.' **Billy McNeil, Celtic captain**

'There is not a prouder man on God's Earth than me at this moment. Winning was important, but it was the way that we won that has filled me with satisfaction. We did it by playing football, pure, beautiful, inventive football. There was not a negative thought in our heads.' **Jock Stein, Celtic manager**

'We can have no complaints. Celtic deserved their victory. We were beaten by Celtic's force. Although we lost, the match was a victory for sport.' **Helenio Herrera, Inter Milan manager**

UEFA CUP FINAL, MAY 2001

Liverpool 5 Alavés 4

The 48,000 crowd in Borussia Dortmund's Westfalenstadion for the UEFA Cup

Final witnessed an action-packed game full of drama, incident and a history-making goal! After a dramatic 90 minutes that produced an eight-goal feast the game went into extra time.

Then there were two sending-offs and the first-ever golden goal to decide the final of a UEFA club competition. And, to add to the drama the golden goal was actually an own-goal! Liverpool, already winners of this cup in 1973 and 1976, were appearing in their third final. The UEFA Cup marked Liverpool's return to a European final following a six-year ban after the Heysel Stadium disaster of 1985.

Alavés, having played in Spain's fourth division just 11 years earlier, were making their European debut. With just over three minutes played defender Babbel headed home a McAllister free kick to put the Reds in front. And in the 16th minute Hamann passed across field to fellow midfielder Gerrard who made it 2-0 to Liverpool.

Alavés responded by bringing on Alonso and just minutes after his arrival he had scored with a 26th-minute header from a Contra cross. The Spanish side now looked dangerous and had a number of attempts to level the score until five minutes from halftime when Herrera brought down England striker Owen in the area. McAllister scored from the penalty spot to make it 3-1 at the break.

Liverpool looked like they had control of the game but Alavés came out for the second half with a fighting spirit and it was no surprise when Moreno headed home after 47 minutes to make it 3-2. Just two minutes later the same player hit the equaliser with a free kick that went through Liverpool's defensive wall.

The Reds brought on midfielder Smicer, who had been dropped for McAllister despite being part of their FA Cup-winning side just days earlier. Striker Fowler, on the bench for the FA Cup, also came on as a sub. Less than eight minutes after his arrival Fowler was on the score sheet. His 72nd-minute shot, from a McAllister pass, put Liverpool back in front.

With less than two minutes remaining it looked like Liverpool were winners until a corner was headed in by Cruyff, son of Dutch legend Johan, to make it 4-4 and take the game to extra time.

The first team to score in this period would win the tie on the golden goal rule. The first fright was for Liverpool – but an Alavés effort that hit the back of the net was ruled offside.

Then the task became even more difficult for the Spanish outfit when Magno, already booked for diving, got a second yellow for a two-footed tackle and received his marching orders. There were no goals after the first period of extra time and with ten minutes of the second period gone Karmona got his second yellow of the game and became the second Alavés player sent off. His foul gave Liverpool a free kick that Man of the Match McAllister sent into the area from where it was headed into his own goal by Geli to give Liverpool victory.

Fans around the world had seen a pulsating game and one that meant Liverpool had won a season treble of UEFA, FA and League Cups. The following week Liverpool won their final Premier League game of the season that ensured a place in the Champions League the following campaign.

TEAMS

Liverpool: Sander Westerveld, Markus Babbel, Sami Hyypia, Stéphane Henchoz (Vladimir Smicer 55), Jamie Carragher, Gary McAllister, Dietmar Hamann, Steven Gerrard, Danny Murphy, Emile Heskey (Robbie Fowler 64), Michael Owen (Patrik Berger 78). Unused subs: Pegguy Arphexad, Grégory Vignal, Stephen Wright, Nick Barmby. Manager: Gérard Houllier

Alavés: Martin Herrera, Antonio Karmona, Oscar Téllez, Dan Eggen (Ivan Alonso 22), Cosmin Contra, Delfi Geli, Jordi Cruyff, Ivan Tomic, Hermes Desio, Martin Astudillo (Magno Mocelin 46), Javi Moreno (Pablo 64). Unused subs: Kike, Ibon Begona, Raul Ganan, Jorge Azkoitia. Manager: Mané (José Manuel Esnal)

AFTER THE FINAL WHISTLE...

'When you play in a European Final, you are looking for immortality. People remember who was playing and when you look at programmes from finals you just recall the facts of the game. These boys have produced a game which will be remembered for a long time, and that is thanks to Alavés too.' **Gerard Houllier, Liverpool manager**

'Dortmund has seen a great final and it was possibly the smallest team in the competition that made it great. We played with pride and class to get the score back to 4-4 at the end of normal time.' **Mané, Alavés coach**

'It has not really sunk in yet what we have accomplished. It was a great achievement and what a season we have had. I had no doubts about taking the penalty and perhaps people will begin to forget that I missed at Wembley in 1996 against England.' **Gary McAllister, Liverpool and Scotland midfielder**

WORLD CUP FINAL, JULY 1954

West Germany 3 Hungary 2

West Germany were the undisputed underdogs against a Hungary team that had flattened all opposition before them. The 64,000 fans in Switzerland's Wankdorf Stadium expected to see a total mismatch—instead they watched what became known as the 'miracle of Berne.'

Hungary had not lost a game in their 34 matches since 1950, a sequence that included six draws and the crushing 6-3 defeat of England at Wembley. Followers of the beautiful game agreed that the Hungarians had some of the best players ever, which included Puskas.

The Germans were nothing like the force they would become in later decades, not helped by the fact that there were no professional leagues in their home country. And when Puskas put Hungary ahead after just six minutes and Czibor made it 2-0 two minutes later it looked like the Germans could be in for a second humiliation, having already been hammered 8-3 by their opposition in the group stages of the tournament.

But Morlock after ten and Rahn on 18 surprisingly drew the Germans level, andh to be fair by this time they were matching their opposition. Despite Hungary turning the screw in the second period and keeping the opposition keeper busy, it was the Germans who grabbed a winner six minutes from time when Rahn fired low into the goal.

Puskas looked like he had equalised in the final minute for the 'Magnificent Magyars', but the strike was ruled offside. The victory is widely accepted as a turning point for German football.

TEAMS

West Germany: Toni Turek, Josef Posipal, Werner Liebrich, Werner Kohlmeyer, Horst Eckel, Karl Mai, Max Morlock, Fritz Walter, Helmut Rahn, Ottmar Walter, Hans Schafer. Manager: Sepp Herberger

Hungary: Gyula Grosics, Jeno Buzanszky, Gyula Lóránt, Mihály Lantos, József Bozsik, József Zakarias, Zoltán Czibor, Nándor Hidegkuti, Mihály Tóth, Sándor Kocsis, Ferenc Puskas. Manager: Gusztáv Sebes

AFTER THE FINAL WHISTLE...

'My usual role was as an attacking wide player, right behind Fritz [Walter]. But in the final I was played deeper in midfield because Hidegkuti normally played behind the strikers and in that area of the pitch. No other coach in the world understood the Hungarian system, much less found a way to beat it, except for one. That was our Sepp Herberger.' **Horst Eckel, German forward**

'Sepp Herberger, who we all simply knew as "Chief", was the father of our success.' **Fritz Walter, West Germany captain**

EURO CHAMPIONSHIPS SEMI-FINAL, JUNE 2000

France 2 Portugal 1

All eyes in this game were on two of Europe's most highly rated footballers of the day— Zinedine Zidane and Luis Figo. Although France captain Deschamps was making his 100th international appearance it was the two midfielders who were under the spotlight. The French knew that if they could reach and then win the final they would become the first team to hold the European Championship and World Cup trophiesat the same time.

Portugal had surprised many by winning all three of their group games, against England, Germany and Romania. They had then despatched Turkey to reach the semis. Their attacking beliefs and form so far in this tournament made them a real threat to France's hopes of a unique double. France, World Cup winners in 1998, had only finished runners-up in their group with wins against Denmark and the Czech Republic and defeat to group winners Holland, before beating Spain in the quarter-inals.

For the first time in European Championship history the semi-finals were held jointly in two countries, Belgium and Holland. A crowd of 47,000 was in Brussels' King Baudouin Stadium to watch this semi-final. France made the better start but it was against the run of play that Portugal took the lead. After 19 minutes Gomes scored after he picked up a ball that had hit a number of players following a shot from Conceicao.

France's players appeared stunned and it took them until the second half to gain some momentum and drag themselves back into the game. Six minutes after the break Thuram passed to Anelka who forwarded the ball to Henry in the penalty area. The Arsenal forward produced one of his typical turns in the box and then fired home the equaliser.

Both sides then found the desire to try and score a winner so that the game did not go to extra time. But the game finished 1-1 at the end of 90 minutes and that meant the two teams would go to an extra half hour, just as they had at the same stage of the competition in 1984. On that occasion France had won 3-2. This time the game had to be settled by a golden goal or a penalty shootout.

France appeared the more determined to grab the first goal that would give them victory, but it took them until three minutes from the end of extra time when Xavier handled a Wiltord shot in the area. The referee decided to give a penalty following discussions with his linesman. Portugal players protested and Figo removed his shirt in disgust before pulling it back over his head and deciding to stay on the pitch.

Zidane, whose form and skills had pushed Figo into the shadows during the game, stepped coolly up to the spot and fired his penalty into the roof of the net to put France into the final. Portugal scorer Gomes continued to protest and was red-carded as he left the field. His manager resigned after the game but claimed it had nothing to do with the result.

France beat Italy 2-1 in the final. Italy took the lead early in the second half but France equalised just before the final whistle to force extra time. David Trezeguet hit the golden goal winner after 103 minutes. Both Figo and Zidane were named in the official team of Euro 2000 but the Frenchman was Player of the Tournament.

TEAMS

France: Fabien Barthez, Bixente Lizarazu, Patrick Vieira, Laurent Blanc, Didier Deschamps, Marcel Desailly, Nicolas Anelka (Sylvain Wiltord 72), Zinedine Zidane, Thierry Henry (David Trezeguet 105), Lilian Thuram, Emmanuel Petit (Robert Pires 87). Unused subs: Bernard Lama, Ulrich Rame, Youri Djorkaeff, Johan Micoud, Frank Leboeuf, Christian Karembeu, Christophe Dugarry. Manager: Roger Lemerre

Portugal: Vitor Baia, Jorge Costa, Vidigal (Paulo Bento 61), Fernando Couto, Luis Figo, Rui Costa (Joao Pinto 78), Sérgio Conceicao, Dimas (Rui Jorge 91), Abel Xavier, Costinha, Nuno Gomes. Unused subs: Pedro Espinha, Quim, Paulo Sousa, Sá Pinto, Beto, Pauleta, Capucho, Secretário. Manager: Humberto Coelho

AFTER THE FINAL WHISTLE…

'It was a shame to go out like that but we played really well and France are a great team. I am not sure it was a penalty or not. Maybe if it had happened against France we would be happy.'**Humberto Coelho, Portugal manager**

'This was a great moment of refereeing. He was just applying the rules. The referee has intervened and the rules must be respected.'**Roger Lemerre, France coach**

'A penalty in extra time with the golden goal rule is a great responsibility but everything went well. When the ball was on the spot I didn't ask myself any questions. I was just concentrating on hitting it hard enough, but it's not always easy to get rid of everything happening around you.' **Zinedine Zidane, France midfielder.**

EUROPEAN CHAMPIONSHIPS FINAL, JULY 2004

Portugal 0 Greece 1

Hosts Portugal were the outright favourites to become European Champions in 2004, but they hadn't bargained for one of the biggest upsets in football history. The Portuguese were not in their best form, but even so the Greeks should have been no match for them in the final of Euro 2004.

The Greeks had other ideas after their stunning progress in this tournament—progress that could only be described as a fairytale. Portugal and Greece had already met at the group stage. Portugal topped the group but lost 2-1 to Greece in the tournament's opening fixture.

Former World Cup holders and reigning European Champions France had been sent packing 1-0 in the quarter-finals by the Greeks. And the highly regarded Czech Republic were no match for the Greek team plan of defending hard and looking for a break. Once again the Greeks won 1-0.

Portugal didn't play pretty football but they proved to be a very impressive side at grinding out results. Portugal had eliminated England in the quarter-finals. They drew 2-2 after extra time and won the penalty shootout 6-5. The much-fancied Holland team were brushed aside 2-1 in the semis. The final wasn't the most inspiring of games. The Greeks' first corner, after 57 minutes, was lofted into the box by Basinas for Charisteas to head home.

The 62,800 crowd in Lisbon's Estádio da Luz had just seen Greece win their first-ever title and become the first nation to win an international championship under the guidance of a foreign manager, German Rehhagel. Rehhagel, at 65 years and 10 months, became the oldest coach to win a European Championship.

TEAMS

Portugal: Ricardo, Miguel (Paulo Ferreira 43), Jorge Andrade, Ricardo Carvalho, Nuno Valente, Maniche, Costinha (Rui Costa 60), Cristiano Ronaldo, Deco, Luis Figo, Pauleta (Nuno Gomes 74) Manager: Luiz Felipe Scolari

Greece: Antonios Nikopolidis, Giourkas Seitaridis, Michalis Kapsis, Traianos Dellas, Takis Fyssas, Kostas Katsouranis, Theodoros Katsouranis, Angelos Basinas, Angelos Charisteas, Stelios Giannakopoulos (Stylianos Venetidis 76), Zisis Vryzas (Dimitrios Papadopoulos 81) Manager: Otto Rehhagel

AFTER THE FINAL WHISTLE...

'We took advantage of our chances. The Greeks have made football history. It's a sensation. The differences between the big teams and the so-called smaller teams have become smaller.' **Otto Rehhagel, Greece coach**

'If we keep working like that then in the future we will win something, but I must congratulate Greece. They have played like this since the beginning of the tournament and they are very good at it. It is up to us to find another way of winning. They have a wonderful defence and it works well. They play on the mistakes of the opponents.' **Luiz Felipe Scolari, Portugal coach**

'We proved once again that the Greek soul is, and always will be, our strength. We are going to take this cup to Greek people all over the world. I think we have given them something more than joy. We have given them a great pride, which they will be able to carry with them for the rest of their lives.' **Theo Zagorakis, Greece captain, Man of the Match in the final**

WORLD CUP SEMI-FINAL, JULY 2014

Brazil 1 Germany 7

Remember the date: July 8, 2014. Those who watched the World Cup semi-final that evening will never forget the result. The stage had been set for what was to be a memorable game. Not one fan or player could have predicted just how memorable. Hosts Brazil had lived on a knife edge from the first game of the finals but with a few slices of luck on their side they had reached the semis. Expectations on home soil had soared. The players simply had to win the World Cup.

But Germany, often criticised for their clinical efficiency, crushed the Samba boys with a style that would have done any Brazilian team of the past proud.

In one of the most incredible international matches ever the Germans slaughtered the hosts 7-1 – Brazil's biggest defeat ever, and their worst since 1920 when they were beaten 6-0 by Uruguay. With ten minutes of the game gone the fixture looked like it could go either way with signs that both sides were up for an attacking game. But then Germany clicked into top gear and the most amazing rout began when Muller side-footed home from just six yards following an eleventh minute corner from Kroos.

Brazil, without suspended captain Thiago Silva and star forward Neymar, looked second-rate and their defence was a total shambles. On 23 minutes keeper Cesar save a shot from Klose but the ball fell back to the striker to hit his side's second. That was Klose's 16th goal at World Cup finals, a new record and ironically one more than the previous best set by Brazil's Ronaldo. The 36-year-old's goal was the first of three in less than three minutes that totally destroyed Brazil and left the home fans booing their own side.. Kroos, provider for the Klose goal, hammered in from 16 yards to make it 3-0 after 24 minutes and grabbed a second less than a minute later after playing a one-two with Khedira. Khedira, one of the stars of this game, got himself on the scoresheet after just 29 minutes after he hit home from 12 yards following a return ball from Ozil.

The half-time whistle blew at 5-0. The Brazilians looked as if they were down and out. Some fans certainly thought they were and left the stadium. The rest of the world eagerly awaited the start of the second half and wondered if any more records would crash in the second period. The fans already knew that Brazil had lost at home for the first time since 1975!

Chelsea forward Schurrle came on after 58 minutes as a sub for the veteran Klose and made sure that his half hour on the pitch was as memorable as the rest of the game. With 69 minutes on the clock the sub smashed home from just eight yards following a cross from Lahm. Ten minutes later Schurrle got a second with a great angled shot.

Germany keeper Neuer didn't have a great deal to do until the dying stages as he kept Brazil at bay with some great saves. But his hopes of a clean sheet were lost with seconds remaining when Oscar grabbed a scant consolation goal. The home side had been totally destroyed. The Germans looked unbeatable on the night whilst the boys from Brazil looked a sad reflection of what football followers would expect from the Samba Boys.

As the conquerors celebrated their march in the final the defeated players wept openly on the pitch. Others had to be comforted by fellow squad members whilst some players bore vacant expressions of disbelief. Television pundits debated what the after effects of this defeat would be on the Brazilian players. Some, they said, may never be the same following this total destruction.

To add to the humiliation, this was the first time Brazil had conceded more than five goals in a World Cup game – even then they had won 6-5 against Poland. It was also the biggest defeat in a World Cup semi-final, the previous worst being when Germany beat Austria 6-1 in 1954. Brazil, five times World Cup winners, had never lost any of their previous six semi-finals in the competition.

TEAMS

Brazil: Julio Cesar, Maicon, Dante, Marcelo, Luiz Gustavo, Fernandinho, (Paulinho 46), Hulk (Ramires 46), Oscar, Bernard, Fred, Willian. Manager: Luiz Felipe Scolari

Germany: Manuel Neuer, Philipp Lahm, Jerome Boateng, Mats Hummels (Per Mertesacker 46), Benedikt Howedes, Bastian Schweinsteiger, Sami Khedira (Julian Draxler 76), Thomas Muller, Toni Kroos, Mesut Ozil, Miroslav Klose (Andre Schurrle 58). Manager: Joachim Low

AFTER THE FINAL WHISTLE...

"I am probably going to be remembered as the coach of Brazil's worst defeat but that was a risk when I took charge 18 months ago. We lost to a great team that had the skill to win the game in six or seven minutes with four goals." **Luiz Felipe Scolari, Brazil coach**

"I remember losing to Italy in the 119th minute in 2006. We know how Scolari and the Brazilian people feel right now. There's never been a result like that, the hosts were unable to deal with the pressure." **Joachim Low, Germany coach.**

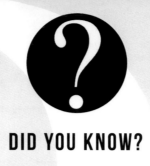

DID YOU KNOW?

- Winger Adam Johnson's five-minute appearance for England against Mexico in May 2010 meant former club Middlesbrough were entitled to a further £1 million in transfer fees from Manchester City. The Blues are believed to have paid £6 million for him in the January 2010 transfer window and sold him to Sunderland in August 2012 for £10 million.

- Striker Gonzalo Higuain could have played for France, where he was born, or for Argentina, the homeland of his father. He walked into the Argentine Embassy in 2009, during his time at Real Madrid, and declared his allegiance to the South Americans.

- Although you are more likely to see England keeper Joe Hart saving penalties, he also loves taking them! He hit the woodwork when he took one for Shrewsbury Town, but scored one for England Under-21s against Sweden in a European Championship shootout.

- England winger Ashley Young has a tattoo that says, 'What doesn't kill you makes you stronger.'

- Wales striker Steve Morison was the first player to score the winning goal in a competitive game at the new Wembley. He hit the winner for Stevenage in their 3-2 victory over Kidderminster Harriers in the 2007 FA Trophy Final.

- When he was a boy, Bulgaria striker Dimitar Berbatov had a No.9 Newcastle

United shirt bearing the name of Alan Shearer—the Premier League's record goal-scorer who twice turned down the chance of joining Man United, one side that Berba did play for!

- Midfielder Gareth Barry became the youngest player to turn out in 300 Premier League matches when he played for Aston Villa against Bolton Wanderers on 28 October 2007 at the age of 26 years and 247 days.

- Former Wigan Athletic keeper Ali Al-Habsi made his debut for Oman while he was still working as an airport fireman! He is now one of his country's most famous sportsmen, having turned out for their international side since 2002 and been the best keeper at five Gulf Cups.

- Liverpool captain and midfielder Steven Gerrard was just nine years old when he started training with the club's youngsters when Kenny Dalglish was manager at Anfield.

- Striker Nicolas Anelka doesn't bother eating his breakfast but when he fancies a burger he'll grab one. 'Even on the eve of a big match I can have broccoli or a burger, it just depends how I feel', admitted the former Bolton, Manchester City, Chelsea and West Brom front man.

CHAPTER 2

BAD BOYS

THE BAD BOYS OF FOOTBALL

Games are often influenced by football's 'bad boys'—and not for the most obvious reasons!

These guys can be front-page headline makers for their antics on and off the pitch, but quite often their teams miss their skills when the players are missing from action for various offences.

Bans, jail sentences, being on loan from their parent club because of problems, or injuries caused by their own rash tackles are all things that have helped these guys miss matches for their teams.

But in a lot of cases the players labelled 'bad boys' are actually more than useful players who can often have a good influence on results. Here are just a few of them…

JOEY Barton

Midfielder Joey Barton was hailed as the 'next big thing' when he arrived on the scene with Manchester City. But his time with the club was cut short after a series of incidents that included a training ground attack on teammate Ousmane Dabo, effectively ending that player's career. Barton later appeared in court, admitted actually bodily harm and was given a four-month suspended jail sentence. Barton also stubbed out a cigar on a City youth player. That led to a £60,000 club fine. He was also caught on TV cameras flashing his backside at Everton fans. City transferred Barton to Newcastle where he missed playing time when he was sent to prison for six months for common assault and affray during a fight in Liverpool. He served 77 days of his sentence and also had to do community work on his release.

Barton moved to QPR on a free transfer for the season 2011–12 but on the final day of that campaign he was sent off at Manchester City for elbowing Carlos Tévez.

As Barton left the pitch he kicked Sergio Aguero, tried to headbutt Vincent Kompany and faced off with Mario Balotelli. The Football Association charged him with violent conduct, handed him a 12-match ban and a £75,000 fine. QPR took the captain's armband from him, fined him around £500,000 and loaned Barton to Marseille for the following season.

Even his own official website declares: 'I'm a footballer, ex-con, ranting anti-celebrity, football's philosopher king, loving dad and violent thug all rolled into one.'

Barton is not afraid to speak his mind and has a vast following on social media site Twitter. He claims: 'A tackle is a tackle. A competitive tackle is a competitive tackle. A fight is a fight. I should know I've had a few!'

'When I was in prison I got £7 a week and that was simpler—you'd use the £7 to buy food', he revealed.

Nigel de Jong

The Holland midfielder's competitive nature has earned him nicknames such as 'The Terrier' and 'Lawnmower.' The former Ajax and Hamburg star was involved in a tackle that put United States midfielder Stuart Holden out of action for two years with a broken leg.

But it was a much higher profile incident that made bigger headlines, and one that even de Jong admits he expected to receive a red card for.

The Dutchman kicked Spain's Xabi Alonso in the chest during the 2010 World Cup Final and referee Howard Webb later admitted, after watching a re-run on television, that if he'd had a better view of the incident he would have sent off the player.

During his time with Manchester City, de Jong was involved in a tackle on Newcastle's Hatem Ben Arfa that put the Frenchman out of action for most of the season.

That incident led to Holland coach Bert van Marwijk banning de Jong from the national side for a period. He said, 'It was a wild and unnecessary offence. I have a problem with the way Nigel needlessly looks to push the limit.'

Marco Materazzi

The Italy defender will forever be remembered as the player head-butted by France legend Zinedine Zidane in the 2006 World Cup Final. But Materazzi, who made almost 500 club appearances, most of them for Inter Milan, and appeared 41 times for his country also has a reputation. His near 18-year career yielded in excess of 60 yellow cards and 25 reds and put him into the top ten list of the world's dirtiest footballers. Four of the sending-offs came in just 27 appearances for Everton.

Diego Maradona

England fans would rate the Argentina forward's highest 'crime' as his 'Hand of God' handball during the 1986 World Cup Finals that led to their side being defeated 2-1.

But the supremely talented footballer also had a few others demons to battle during his career.

Maradona was suspended from football for 15 months in 1991 after failing a drug test for cocaine during his time with Napoli. He was also sent home in disgrace after failing a drug test at the 1994 World Cup Finals. Maradona, who had played in two games, claimed a banned substance was in a power drink he had consumed. But his dismissal from the tournament also saw an end to his international career of 91 games and 34 goals.

Felipe Melo

Melo is a skilled midfielder whose darker side earned him the title of 'Pit bull' among Galatasaray fans. But before he had arrived at the Turkish side he'd already been building up a dossier of shame.

Melo stamped on Holland winger Arjen Robben and was sent off in the 2010 World Cup quarter-finals. After the game Melo said, 'Robben kept playing up. If I meant to hurt him, he would have left the pitch. I have enough strength to break his leg.'

The following year, playing for Juventus, Melo was red-carded for another horror attack, this time on Parma's Massimo Paci. Paci had tackled Melo and then fallen to the ground, where the Brazilian kicked Paci in the face. That incident led to Melo moving to Turkey where he became a cult hero among Galatasaray fans, although he probably didn't help his own cause when he said, 'I'm the team's pit bull. I run, I chase down and I bite my opponents.'''

NUMBERS GAME

Some shirt numbers are iconic. Others are created for strange or sentimental reasons…

3

AC Milan's one-club defender Paolo Maldini turned out a staggering 902 times for the Rossoneri and in 126 games for Italy. When he retired in 2009 his club shirt was also taken out of service—although if any of his two children turn out for the club the player has been given permission to pass the No.3 onto them.

6

Bobby Moore, arguably the most famous player in England and West Ham history, wore the No.6 at Upton Park. It is unlikely that another West Ham player will earn the same adoration from both his club fans and England supporters, with Moore having lifted the World Cup on home soil in 1966. Moore served club and country with distinction and his famed club shirt was retired in 2008 having last been worn by defender George McCartney.

West Ham chief executive Scott Duxbury revealed: 'When we were talking about ways to mark 50 years since Bobby Moore's debut, there was only one true gesture that would do him justice – retiring the number six shirt he made his own.'

7

Many people regard the No.7 as lucky. In the case of Liverpool fans it stands for skilled players who have pulled on the legendary shirt.

Former England striker Kevin Keegan, player and then manager Kenny Dalglish,

Peter Beardsley, Steve McManaman and Champions League winner Vladimir Smicer have worn the number.

Uruguay striker Luis Suárez, who took on the seven when he arrived at Anfield in 2011, admits, 'I hadn't realised its history when I asked for the seven. Now I'm quite happy that I did. Now I know about players like Kenny Dalglish and Kevin Keegan.'

Five of the best and most memorable players ever to grace Manchester United's Old Trafford turf have pulled on the number seven. Perhaps the most famous was Irishman George Best who left a lasting impression on anyone who witnessed his amazing skills.

England midfielder Bryan Robson was labelled 'Captain Fantastic' during his time wearing the number.

Frenchman Eric Cantona was more arrogant, but his fantastic abilities made him another Red Devils legend and his arrival at the club marked an upturn in its fortunes.

Former England captain David Beckham made the number his own with his crisp passing before Cristiano Ronaldo created more memories ahead of his world-record £80 million move to Real Madrid in 2009.

Albie Morgan, United's kitman, said, 'I can remember David Beckham when Eric left – he was desperate for that number seven shirt, absolutely desperate, and he did very well in it when he got it. We've been blessed with these great number sevens who know how to lead men both on and off the pitch, set an example to their team mates and consistently score important goals.'

9

The traditional shirt of the centre forward and in the case of Newcastle United, the most iconic number at the club.

Worn by the likes of Jackie Milburn, Hughie Gallacher, Malcolm McDonald, Andy Cole and Premier League record scorer Alan Shearer, the No.9 must be worn with pride and distinction at St. James' Park.

Shearer, who scored 206 goals for Newcastle in the decade he pulled on the No.9, said, 'It's a fantastic shirt. It's a great honour and privilege to wear it but you can be scared of it because of what has gone before – not just the goals I scored, the Macdonalds, [Les] Ferdinand and others.'

Ferdinand wore the No.9 for one season, 1995–96, before agreeing to hand over the shirt when local hero Shearer joined Newcastle in a then world-record £15 million transfer.

10

The number worn by Diego Maradona was retired when he left Napoli in 1992, having helped the Italians to two Serie A titles, Italian Cup and Italian Supercup in eight years.

Attempts by Argentina to also retire the forward's number were turned down by FIFA, world football's governing body.

The shirt of Roma's record goal scorer and most-capped Italy striker Francesco Totti is set to be retired when the player's contract with the club runs out in 2016, just short of his 40th birthday.

10

Tottenham fans demand entertaining football and they certainly got that when England midfielder Glenn Hoddle pulled on the No.10. They have also had goals galore from their number tens, who have included England's Gary Lineker, goal machine Jimmy Greaves and Republic of Ireland record scorer Robbie Keane.

Hoddle said: 'Often the No.10 shirt was worn by a striker, like Gary Lineker. To me, ten was the shirt that stood for creativity and ability; a player who can open a game with a pass, with either foot, or score a decisive goal. I first wore it for the under 11s and for the school team and later for Tottenham's first team.'

14

Amsterdam giants Ajax retired their number 14 shirt in 2007 in honour of Holland legend Johan Cruyff. The club hung up the jersey on the eve of the midfielder's 60th birthday to respect a player who was with them from 1964 to 1973 and from 1981 to 1983.

Ajax chairman John Jaakke said, 'Johan Cruyff has been of priceless value to Ajax and gave the club its world-wide reputation.'

23

David Beckham wore this number after he moved from Manchester United to Real Madrid and then on to LA Galaxy. He chose the number because he was a fan of basketball legend Michael Jordan, who had the numbers on his own shirt. There were suggestions Beckham could have had four or 23 when he arrived in Madrid. He plumped for 23 after wife Victoria revealed it was Jordan's number.

39

France striker Nicolas Anelka wore this number during his time at Manchester City, and also at Fenerbahce, Bolton Wanderers, Chelsea, Shanghai Shenhua and West Brom. The former Arsenal number nine insisted on wearing the 39 when he moved clubs, having first picked it up at Manchester City where nine, 19 and 29 were already taken.

Anelka wore 39 for France but had to accept 18 when he joined Juventus on loan in 2013.

BA HUMBUG…

Senegal striker Demba Ba isn't a player who worries about his shirt number. He wore 9 and 29 at Hoffenheim, 21 at West Ham and 19 at Newcastle United and Chelsea.

END OF ERAS

Many shirts are 'retired from duty' in memory of players who have died.

Manchester City shelved the number 23 in memory of Marc-Vivien Foé, who was on loan to the Citizens from Lyon when he died while playing for Cameroon.

Among other shirts hung up posthumously; Chievo gave up their No.30 when DR Congo forward Jason Mayélé was killed in a car crash in 2002 while on his way to catch the team bus for an away game.

Benfica retired the 29 when their striker Miklos Feher died of a cardiac arrest during a match against Vitoria de Guimaraes in 2004. He had played 25 games for Hungary and scored seven goals.

FANS HONOURED

Many teams do not issue the number 12 to a player but dedicate it to their supporters, 'the twelfth man.' It is a common practice in Japan and in Brazil. Brazilian sides, however, have to issue the number to players in their CONMEBOL competitions' squads who have to be numbered one to 25!

FOOTBALLERS' DAYS OFF

What do stars get up to when they are not training or playing the game?

LET'S HEAR IT FOR THE BOYS

Morten Gamst Pedersen is more famous in his home country of Norway than his country's king!

With four other footballers he formed boy band The Players, who had a No.1 hit in their homeland with *This Is For Real.* They donated their profits to a charity called Soccer Against Crime.

Striker Roque Santa Cruz, who like Pedersen played in the English Premier League with Blackburn, scored a Top 40 hit in Austria and Germany when he sang with the rock band Sportfreunde Stiller.

DAILLY DOSE

Former Scotland defender Christian Dailly was lead singer and guitarist in powerpop-indie rock band South Playground, formed with three friends. The ex-West Ham and Rangers star has even heard his most famous song, *Scale Free*, played over the loudspeakers at Hampden Park.

RACING CERTAINTY

Former England striker Michael Owen is horseracing mad! He is friends with champion jockey Frankie Dettori and now Michael has retired from football he even has his own stables where he plans to groom winners. The Owen family are often spotted at race meetings and Michael got a bit carried away once while he was in a Newcastle betting shop watching one of his horses in a race. 'When she won I couldn't help myself, I just opened the door of the bookies and ran up and down the street', admitted Michael.

The first horse the former Liverpool, Real Madrid, Newcastle, Manchester United and Stoke star owned was called Etienne Lady, named after the city Saint-Étienne in France where Owen scored his famous World Cup goal against Argentina in 1998.

TABLE TOPPER

Robin van Persie's a star when it comes to playing with a ball far smaller than the one he is more usually associated with. The Man United and Holland striker is a smash hit at table tennis. He is so good that he got an invite to take part in a celebrity event at London's swish Albert Hall.

KEEPER SHOOTS…

Veteran keeper Steve Harper is a sports fanatic. Harps likes to take in a round of golf with his former Newcastle team mates Shay Given and Alan Shearer; is qualified to referee at lower football games and is also useful with a cricket bat. But watch out when Harps, who played for Hull in 2013–14, takes aim at a dartboard! He's a hotshot with the arrows and even gave darts ace Phil 'The Power' Taylor a run for his money in an exhibition game.

REVEALED…

- USA international midfielder Clint Dempsey, who had a spell with Fulham, is also known as rapper Deuce. He has a video on YouTube called 'Don't Tread', featuring Big Hawk and XO.
- Inter Milan-bought Republic of Ireland striker Robbie Keane in 2000 for £13

million from Coventry City—a transfer fee that means he cost them £1 million for every game in which he played!

- Defender Stephen Warnock was on the bench for England's friendly against Brazil—but when the FA rang him to say he had been selected by manager Fabio Capello, the player had his mobile on silent and missed the call!

- Mathew Mitchel-King, a defender with Crewe Alexandra, was Rio Ferdinand's official body double when sports giants Nike shot adverts. Former Manchester United and England defender Ferdinand wasn't allowed to risk injury in photo shoots.

- England striker Darren Bent got into a spot of bother when he used Twitter to criticise Tottenham who stalled on his transfer to Sunderland. He's now stopped Tweeting…

- Actor Matt Smith, who played Doctor Who in the BBC TV worldwide hit, was once scouted by Leicester City, then of the Premier League, but a back injury ended his hopes of playing.

- When Andriy Arshavin scored four goals for Arsenal against Liverpool he swapped shirts with Anfield striker Fernando Torres. He then sent the Spain international's kit back to his coach at former club Zenit Saint Petersburg who collected No.9 shirts!

- England bosses Steve McClaren and Fabio Capello picked John Terry as their captain—and six Chelsea bosses have also handed the defender the armband. Claudio Ranieri was first to give him the job, followed by Jose Mourinho, Avram Grant, Luiz Felipe Scolari, Guus Hiddink then Carlo Ancelotti.

- The first football shirt owned by England and Manchester United midfielder Tom Cleverley was a Nottingham Forest one, because of his dad Andrew's allegiance to the side. But it wasn't long before the youngster had a Bradford City strip and season ticket as he trained with the team as a schoolboy.

- Tim Howard was the first North American player to pick up an FA Cup winner's medal when Manchester United beat Millwall 3-0 in 2004. The keeper left Old Trafford to join Everton.

- Norway striker John Carew is a fan of seriously big and fast cars! Among the prized motors owned by the former Valencia and Aston Villa front man are a Lamborghini, Porsche and an orange-coloured Dodge Charger.

- When he was a youngster, former England keeper David James earned money by cutting grass so that he could buy a pair of the same gloves worn by legendary Italy keeper Dino Zoff.

- Liverpool midfielder Steven Gerrard made his England debut the day after his 20th birthday, but it was 16 months before he scored his first senior goal, in the Three Lions' famous 5-1 victory in Germany. He has since become captain for club and country.

- Frank Lampard's Chelsea teammates nicknamed him 'The Professor' after a test discovered he has a very high IQ.

DID YOU KNOW?

- Top players queued up to learn some new tricks—from magician Dynamo. He was even invited round to Michael Owen's house to put on a show for the former England striker and Manchester United stars Wayne Rooney and Tom Cleverley. Football fan Dynamo also worked with the league's sponsors Barclays and amazed Jermain Defoe, Jermaine Jenas; Bobby Zamora, Philippe Senderos, Rio Ferdinand, Nani, Nemanja Vidic and former Old Trafford defender Gary Neville.

- If Manchester City had moved earlier to buy Bosnia striker Edin Dzeko they could have landed him for a cut-price fee. He was available for £18.5 million, the amount in a release clause, but then he signed a new deal with Wolfsburg and when the Blues bought him in January 2011 he cost £27 million!

- When defender Gary Cahill, then at Bolton, scored against Bulgaria in September 2011, he became the first Wanderers player since Nat Lofthouse 52 years earlier to hit the back of the net for England.

- Striker Peter Crouch won a Champions League loser's medal with Liverpool in 2007 but keeps it hidden behind the FA Cup winner's medal he won with the club the previous year.

- South Korea midfielder Park Ji-sung was still at university when he was offered a professional deal in Japan with his first club. He later won two Dutch titles and a Dutch Cup with PSV Eindhoven, plus four Premier League titles, three League

Cups and European Cup with Manchester United.

- When midfielder Jamie O'Hara was house hunting in the Midlands following his move from Tottenham to Wolves he spotted a big property with its own lake where he could go fishing. Instead, he chose to settle for a home just a short distance from one of the best fishing lakes in the area!

- Gareth Bale, the world's most expensive player, is teetotal. The Real Madrid and former Tottenham star tried a beer and didn't like the taste, so his Man of the Match champagne awards are left untouched.

- Winger Jermaine Pennant admitted that after training in Spain, during his time with Real Zaragoza, he went home and watched TV—which he didn't understand—or played on his Xbox for eight hours at a time. Pennant was disciplined three times for turning up late to training, following which he never played for the Spanish side again and was sold to Stoke City.

- It took midfielder Scott Parker eight years to win his first eight England caps— and his first four came while playing for four different clubs.

- He made his debut as a sub in February 2003 while at Charlton and turned out for the side again from the bench the following March after a move to Chelsea.

- In October 2006, he made his first start for England during his time at Newcastle United and in November 2008 he turned out for the Three Lions having moved to West Ham. In 2011, the same year he moved to Tottenham, he was England fans' Player of the Year.

- Defender Danny Simpson has two Championship winner's medals, both with rival teams! He won one with Sunderland in 2007 during a loan from Manchester United and got his other in 2010 after a permanent transfer to Newcastle United.

- Striker Danny Welbeck still qualified to play for Ghana—even after turning out for England against that country in March 2011. As that game was a friendly it meant the Manchester United forward was still able to change his mind. But when he finally pulled on the Three Lions shirt for the game against Montenegro in October 2011 that committed him to the England cause.

- Frank Lampard is the highest scoring midfielder ever to play in the Premier League. He scored 251goals during his career in England before leaving Chelsea in 2014, a total not likely to be beaten by anyone in his position.

- When Alex Oxlade-Chamberlain made his full England debut, he and dad Mark became only the fifth father and son partnership to have turned out for the Three Lions. The others are the Lampards (Frank junior and senior), Brian and Nigel Clough, the Easthams (both George) and Ian Wright and his adopted son Shaun Wright-Phillips.

- Striker Sergio Aguero loves eating steak, but he had to enlist the help of fellow Argentines Carlos Tevez and Pablo Zabaleta to find out where to buy meat imported from his home country when he signed for Manchester City in 2011.

CHAPTER 3

FIGHT CLUB!

WHEN PLAYERS SCRAP

There are some players—and managers—that you shouldn't mess with…

KEANE BATTLER

Former Republic of Ireland star Roy Keane really did live up to his tag of a midfield battler!

The ex-Manchester United captain never shirked a challenge and even had bust-ups with other skippers, including a tunnel fracas with Arsenal and France midfielder Patrick Vieira.

Keane was also red-carded for decking Newcastle striker Alan Shearer, elbowing Jason McAteer of Sunderland, and for stamping on Gareth Southgate of Crystal Palace.

By his own admission, Keane went out for payback against Norway's Alf-Inge Haaland four years after the player had injured him during a game against Leeds! Keane deliberately put his boot into Haaland's knee to end his season and was fined £150,000. Haaland was by then playing for United's rivals Man City.

CLOUGH'S CLOUT

Straight-talking manager Brian Clough didn't hold back on what he said—or his punches in one case! When some so-called fans invaded Nottingham Forest's City Ground following a victory against QPR, Clough was not impressed. He went after three of the invaders and punched one of them, which led to a touchline ban and meant he had to watch games from the stand for the rest of the season.

HIGHLAND FLING!

When someone is 1.93m (6ft 4in) tall and carries the reputation of a fearsome Scotsman you wouldn't really mess with him, would you? In fact, if you knew the guy was a fit professional footballer who had already served a jail sentence for assaulting a player during a game you would definitely back off. The two burglars who broke into the home of Everton and Scotland striker Duncan Ferguson obviously didn't think much of his hard-man reputation.

One did escape—although he was later caught—but the other burglar was pinned to the ground by Big Dunc until the police arrived. The would-be housebreaker who was nicked also spent a few days in hospital…

WHEN TEAMMATES CLASH

Fans, players and managers had to look twice when they saw Lee Bowyer and Kieron Dyer fighting…the two were on the same side! The midfielders were turning out for Newcastle but turned on each other when their side went 3-0 down to Aston Villa in a home game in 2005. Bowyer's shirt was ripped and the pair were sent off after they had to be separated by opposition midfielder Gareth Barry. Both Newcastle stars were banned for three games for their red cards. Bowyer was later fined £30,000 by the Football Association and given an additional three-game ban. He was also fined six weeks' wages by Newcastle.

Bowyer appeared in court in connection with the brawl and admitted using threatening behaviour. That resulted in another fine of £600 plus £1,000 costs.

Dyer escaped a fine as it was ruled he had not thrown the first punch.

Newcastle manager Graeme Souness also forced the pair to issue a public apology.

CHOP, CHOP…

When fans and pundits labelled Frenchman Eric Cantona eccentric they weren't wrong!

The Manchester United forward was banned for four months and fined £30,000 for launching a kung-fu kick at a Crystal Palace fan. Cantona had just been sent off at Palace's Selhurst Park ground when he took exception to comments from home fan Matthew Simmonds.

Later Cantona claimed: 'When I did the kung-fu kick on the hooligan, because these kind of people don't have to be at the game, I think maybe it's like a dream for some, you know sometimes to kick these kind of people.'

Cantona had prior bans for punching his own team's keeper during his time at Auxerre and being suspended by Marseille for kicking a ball into the crowd and throwing his shirt at the referee!

TARTAN TERROR

Local rivalry doesn't come much stronger than in Glasgow where Rangers and Celtic both play their games.

And Celtic boss Neil Lennon knows more than most what it's all about, having received death threats, a bullet and parcel bombs in the post! He also had to dodge a flying fist when a fan ran at him during a game with Hearts.

PARD LUCK

Alan Pardew looks the part in his smart suits and ties and neatly combed hair. But a few players and managers have discovered you don't get on the wrong side of this gaffer…

Pardew was fined £100,000 by his own club, Newcastle United, in March 2014 for going to head butt Hull City player David Meyler during an away game. They also warned him about his future conduct.

The Football Association charged the boss with improper conduct and fined him another £60,000.

Pardew, who admitted the charge, was also given a seven-match ban. For the first three of those games he wasn't allowed to contact any member of his team or coaching staff an hour before kick-off and wasn't allowed into the stadium.

For the next four banned games he wasn't allowed onto the touchline and was forced to watch from the stands.

'I deeply regret the incident and wholeheartedly apologise to all parties for my conduct, which I understand was not acceptable', Pardew said after an FA hearing.

Previously, Pardew had received a two-match touchline ban and £20,000 fine for pushing an assistant linesman during the opening game of 2012–13 against Tottenham.

And he got a ticking off from the FA when he launched a foul-mouthed tirade against Manchester City boss Manuel Pellegrini in January 2014.

PUSHING ON

Former England midfielder Paul Ince was banned from being in the stadium for five Blackpool games after pushing the fourth official.

Ince, the Seasiders' manager at the time, was said to have 'violently' shoved the official and hurled abused at him after a 2-1 win over Bournemouth in September 2013.

Ince had already been sent to the stands for throwing a bottle that hit a female fan.

Stewards and players had to restrain the boss as he threatened to 'knock out' the fourth official, according to referee Oliver Langford.

Ince, who thought the ban was 'very, very harsh' added: 'The push was not aggressive; only enough to move him away from where I was, only in order to avoid a real possibility of a one-to-one confrontation. I know I should not have pushed him and I wholeheartedly apologise.'

CITY 9,000 TOWN 18,000

Bradford City and Crawley Town were both fined following a brawl that broke out at the end of their League 2 game. The on-field punch-up involved 22 players and resulted in five red cards been issued in the dressing rooms AFTER the game!

Bradford were later fined £9,000 by the Football Association and Crawley £18,000.

CLATTERED

Lee Cattermole, the Premier League's second most sent off player, played 73 games in the top-flight before getting his first red card. He's received his marching orders so many times that he earned the nickname Clattermole! But without a doubt his most embarrassing red card came in Sunderland's derby game at Newcastle in March 2012 when Cattermole was booked within the first minute—and got his second yellow AFTER the final whistle. He had an altercation with referee Mike Dean in the tunnel as the players left the pitch at the end of the game, and his second card that meant he had been sent off!

BALLED BOY

Former England defender Gary Neville, now a punter with Sky Sports, was sent off whilst playing for Manchester United when he kicked the ball at an Everton fan who had been giving him stick!

PAYING THE PRICE

A few of the crazy fines to hit football players and clubs

CRUNCH FOR CARLOS

Striker Carlos Tevez filled the coffers at Manchester City with a whole series of fines.

The Argentina star's problems began following bizarre scenes in Germany where he refused to take to the pitch as a substitute during the club's Champions League clash with Bayern Munich. Tevez was initially handed a fine of two weeks' wages—around £400,000—but was handed another fine of six weeks' pay—£1.2 million—for gross misconduct.

Two months after the Munich madness, Tevez flew home to Argentina without permission from the club and remained in his home country for months. He returned to the City squad for the final few games of the season but the whole incident cost Tevez around £9.3 million in lost wages, fines and bonuses.

SHOT DOWN

England defender Ashley Cole has had a number of crazy fines but the one he was hit with in 2011 was the most bizarre. The England defender was made to pay £250,000 for accidentally shooting a student who was on a work experience placement with Chelsea. Cole had been holding an air rifle at the club's Surrey training ground and showing it off to teammates.

A year earlier, the left-back was reportedly fined £200,000 by club owner Roman Abramovich for twice smuggling a girl into the team hotel after away matches and 'tarnishing the image of the club.'

DOWN THE TOILET

Wales midfielder Robbie Savage was fined two weeks' wages for using the referee's toilet in the match officials' changing room. Savage, then playing for Leicester City against Aston Villa, has since referred to the 2002 incident as one of the more bizarre moments of his career! The rules state that players cannot enter the officials' room without permission. Savage, who claimed he was suffering from a stomach upset, ran to the nearest vacant facilities due to the fact the toilets in his side's dressing room were in use.

The Football Association fined Savage after he was found guilty of improper conduct.

SEAT OF PROBLEM

A toilet seat landed England full back Glen Johnson with an £80 fine in 2007. Johnson was accused of trying to steal the seat from a local hardware store and was handed an on-the-spot fine by police. He later claimed he had gone to the shop with a friend who bought a bathroom set: 'But it didn't have a slow close toilet seat so he changed it over then we went to pay. We didn't know this toilet seat was £3 more expensive until the guy said, so we offered to pay the difference.

The guy was buzzin' to make a scene and called the police. What sort of thieves go through the checkout to pay? Come on!'

PAY UP!

- Manchester City were fined nearly £25,000 for being ONE minute late back onto the pitch for the start of the second half of their Europa League game against Sporting Lisbon in 2012.
- Portugal forward Cristiano Ronaldo was fined £8,000 by boss Sir Alex Ferguson for constantly sending text messages during training sessions while he was at Manchester United.
- Middlesbrough were fined £50,000 and docked three points for calling off a game at Blackburn with 24 hours' notice in 1997. The lost points led to them

being relegated from the Premier League.

- Seventeen players from Kuala Lumpur FA, who were playing in the country's third tier, were fined for match fixing.

- A sign at Arsenal's training ground in 2012–13 the season said players would be fined £500 for using their mobile phone in the building—although texting was allowed!

- Tottenham appealed against a £600,000 FA fine in 1994 and were landed with an increased payment of £1.2 million. Spurs had been found guilty of illegal payment to players in an FA Cup game.

STARS WHO ROCK!

The beautiful game's links to the world of music…

LOVE THEM DO…1

Former Beatle Paul McCartney, one of the richest pop stars in the world, has claimed he supports both Merseyside teams, Liverpool and Everton. But when push comes to shove Macca admits that he favours blue over red and will sing the praises of Everton. The proud Liverpudlian singer and guitarist reckons he has to pledge his allegiance to both sides as they are based in his home city. But with his father born in the Everton area and all of his close family Evertonians there is only one side that gets Macca's support when the two giants face each other!

LOVE THEM DO…2

Sami Hyypia got in the spirit of things when he arrived at Liverpool by deciding to brush up on tunes by The Beatles. The Finland defender, who spent ten years at

Anfield, reckoned the Fab Four were one of his favourite groups and should be a must-listen for anyone on Merseyside. Hyypia admitted to having 'loads' of their songs on his iPod and that he knew all of the words to hit *Yellow Submarine*!

ONE TRIES

Doncaster Rovers' reserves are more used to being watched by a handful of diehard supporters and maybe the odd dog—but that changed when a pop star turned out for the side. The debut of Louis Tomlinson from boy band One Direction saw pop fans from all over Europe travel to South Yorkshire in England to see him pull on a shirt for the first time. Tomlinson, signed by the club on a non-contract basis almost six months earlier, came on as a substitute in front of more than 4,000 fans—compared to the usual 100 or so at reserve games.

Although the game against local rivals Rotherham ended 0-0, a local children's hospice were big winners from ticket sales.

'This has always been a childhood dream for me', said Tomlinson. 'I feel very honoured to have been asked to sign for Rovers and being able to help both the club and the amazing charity Bluebell Wood is what it's all about.'

Meanwhile, fellow One Direction star Niall Horan was given the thumbs up to train with Premier League side Chelsea. Blues' boss Jose Mourinho gave the OK after meeting the singer when he went with his daughter to a 1-D concert.

Horan got onto the same pitch as the star-studded first team but wasn't allowed to train with the big-name players.

DUDE'S NOT CRAZY

Although Brian Johnson, lead singer with world renowned rock group AC/DC, now lives in America he still regularly follows the fortunes of home town team Newcastle United. The Geordie, once linked to buying the St. James' Park club, has followed the side in black and white stripes since he was a boy.

Johnno admitted to a local radio station: 'It wasn't so much buying it, Jackie Milburn [the club's legendary striker] took me to see the committee, the Board, and I was very excited about doing it and then about halfway through we both looked at each other and both realised they wanted me to put in—this was about 1981 or 82—half a million pounds, which at the time was a fortune.

For that they were going to make me an honorary board member with no decisions and no say. I realised that it was just a big, big stitch up by these greedy men who wanted more money from some silly pop star dude.'

THEY WERE ON FIRE!

Kasabian made history when they became the first rock band to launch an England football shirt.

The group revealed the Three Lions' red away shirt from Umbro in front of thousands of fans at the Paris Olympia theatre.

Frontman Tom Meighan wore the shirt, which the England team wore at the 2010 World Cup finals in South Africa, as the band belted out their song *Fire*.

'It was brilliant to be the first band ever to launch an England shirt and where better to launch this particular kit than away from home?' asked Tom.

"We jumped at the chance as we are all football fans and loved the idea of revealing the England away shirt when playing in the country of one of our great footballing rivals.' Umbro selected Brit winners Kasabian because the group is a fan of Leicester City.

SCOT ON TAPE

Many footballers fancy themselves as singers—but Kevin Rutkiewicz went a few steps further.

The Scottish Premier League defender wrote and recorded his own album *Handwritten* and toured with Midge Ure, former singer with Ultravox and one of the driving forces behind Live Aid.

Kevin picked up the guitar while out of action with injury at Aberdeen and during a spell at St. Johnstone he was invited to play a charity concert.

Kevin, who has also turned out for Dunfermline, played the King Tut's Wah Wah Hut venue in his native Glasgow.

RING TONE

Former Newcastle and Aston Villa winger Nobby Solano formed his own Salsa band! The Peru midfielder who also had spells with West Ham and Hull City also had a musical prank he worked on former Toon Army boss Sir Bobby Robson: 'I used to phone up his mobile and play my trumpet down the phone to him. He didn't know it was me, but one day somebody told him that I knew how to play the trumpet. So then he worked out it must be me, called me up and just laughed with me down the phone.'

GO ON PUNK...

Tomas Rosicky could really make the fans' day off the pitch—as he has played guitar for a punk rock group! The Arsenal midfielder picked up the electric axe during the Czech Republic's Footballer of the Year ceremony to play with Lou Fananek Hagen and his band Tri Sestry.

The crowd reckoned he was pretty good and Rosicky has since practised his plucking for a possible career after football!

ANDY THE STRUMMER

Andy Reid has pulled strings in a few teams' midfields—and he's handy when it comes to pulling them on a guitar. The former Republic of Ireland star, who has turned out for Nottingham Forest, Tottenham, Sunderland and Blackpool, admitted: 'I have written some songs but not many people get to hear them. I don't think many will! I think some are OK; some are pretty poor. I am certainly not recording any while I play football. Afterwards, who knows what will happen?'

TRUE BLUES

Brothers Noel and Liam Gallagher—who founded rock group Oasis—have great trouble agreeing on anything…except their love of Manchester City. They are regulars at games although when City played Wigan in the 2013 FA Cup Final the pair went to the game separately.

The younger Liam also shares his brother's hatred of all things Manchester United and instead of autographing a guitar for Red Devils' legend Gary Neville he scratched City's MCFC initials on the instrument.

Noel did a similar trick when he was asked to autograph a guitar for United striker Wayne Rooney. He sent a light blue—city's colours—guitar to the forward and wrote on it: 'Happy Birthday Fat Boy.'

Liam even gate-crashed a City press conference when his side went top of the Premier League and asked journalists what they wanted to know!

QUICK TUNES...

- Man United and England striker Wayne Rooney is known to have a pretty wide choice of favourite music—some not so great—but he's also reportedly keen on learning how to drum!

- England forward Joe Cole started to learn guitar during his time at Chelsea. The midfielder took lessons from Patrick Mascall, multi-talented strummer with rock group Van Tramp.

- Sunderland defender Titus Bramble and battling midfielder Lee Cattermole became big mates with Take That star Robbie Williams after meeting up with him in America. Evidently the Robster's singing is better than his football…

DID YOU HEAR?

- 'It's the last thing I want to do. I just don't watch football. I get home, I switch off because it is everywhere and it's all everyone wants to talk about.' Former QPR, Brighton, West Ham, Fulham and England striker Bobby Zamora prefers to go fishing. Honest!

- 'Opinions are like backsides, we've all got them but it's not always wise to air them in public.' Mick McCarthy, then Wolves boss, responds to Joey Barton ranting on Twitter.

- 'Who would I rather be, captain of Liverpool or Bond? I don't think I could keep up any more, so Bond – but Steven Gerrard would make a good Bond. He is a good leader.' 007 actor Daniel Craig gives Stevie G a licence to thrill.

- 'When I joined Villa I didn't know where they played. I thought they were a London club!' Good job Belgium striker Christian Benteke wasn't asked to make his own way to Birmingham-based Villa!

- 'We showed we are not a one-trick monkey.' Was Newcastle United boss Alan Pardew taking the pony!

- 'One day the ball knocked my front teeth out and my mum wouldn't let me play as a keeper anymore.' Now you know why Fernando Torres became a striker for Atletico Madrid, Liverpool, Chelsea and Spain!

- 'The first thing he said was, "You guys listen to me and you will win every game".' No surprise that Rafael van der Vaart is talking about his former Real Madrid boss Jose Mourinho.

- 'He was training with a steak in his boot. He didn't' play with it because we were worried it might get a bit hot and start cooking.' Aston Villa No.2 Peter Grant revealed how the club tried to beef up the performances of defender James Collins…

- 'Sometimes we looked like headless chickens running around after the ball.' Defender Daniel Agger cries fowl after Liverpool were held to a goal-less draw by Swansea.

- 'I feel physically sick. Anyone watching that would think it's like a pub team really. It's unacceptable. I'm embarrassed walking past those supporters of ours who've travelled all that way to watch absolute garbage,' Boss Paul Jewell wasn't happy when his Ipswich side lost 4-0 to Burnley!

- 'We drew the game he played but I decided not to play him in the next game because his warm up had consisted of two bottles of Budweiser and three cigarettes.' Club owner Simon Clifford reveals why Brazil legend Socrates didn't get more than one game for his non-league Garforth Town.

- 'I catch myself calling my kids dude once in a while and using American words like elevator instead of lift.' Living in the USA got to former England captain David Beckham.

- 'I've learnt probably more tonight than I have in the other games. I don't think you learn much about your players when you're winning games.' Manager Neil Warnock comes up with a new line after his Leeds side were beaten 7-3 at home to Nottingham Forest.

- 'He's got a big nine-inch gap on his head and about 14 stitches! That's just a scratch to him – he's fine.' Boss Alan Pardew reveals why Newcastle's Ivory Coast midfielder Cheick Tiote is rated as a hard man!

- 'A few of us practised penalties on Friday and I thought "it's never going to come to me". I was joking that I'd volunteer to take the 11th.' …and then Huddersfield keeper Alex Smithies was asked to take the eleventh spot-kick in the penalty shootout and gained his side promotion in the 2012 League One play-off final.

CHAPTER 4

SECRETS OF THE STARS

Check out some things you may not have heard about top players!

TUNED IN

The Ferdinand brothers were hooked on totally different television characters when they were youngsters. Older brother, England and former Manchester United defender Rio, admitted to a liking for silly scarecrow character Wurzel Gummidge. While Anton, also a defender, who played for West Ham, Sunderland and QPR before a move to Turkey, went for the more robust The Incredible Hulk!

LICKING GOOD

Legendary Chelsea defender John Terry likes to win at everything, whether it's football, darts or fishing. But his teammates know that they are likely to be splattered big time if he takes them paintballing! They reckon he gets stuck in to the game as much as he does to attackers on the pitch.

HE'S REALLY MOTORING

Everyone knew when Wayne Rooney put his £150,000 Aston Martin Vanquish up for sale—it was advertised in the pages of a car magazine. The England and Manchester United forward flogged the motor so that he could buy a Mercedes McLaren SLF Roadstar—yet he had just signed a sponsorship deal that saw him get a six-litre Merc worth more than £120,000.

Having signed a new United deal in 2014 that was worth a reported £300,000 a week he might just have enough to buy whatever car he wants…

BRUSH STROKES

Former Hull City and Republic of Ireland striker Caleb Folan brushed up on some new skills ready for life after playing.

'I like to do different things away from football', he admitted.

The former Wigan hit man added: 'I'm into design, like fashion design and painting. I like the modern stuff like the graffiti artist Banksy. It keeps me occupied and kind of brings me to a calm place when I am not playing and takes my mind off football.'

SMASHING STRIKER

England and Arsenal striker Theo Walcott is rated as a smashing player—but many fans probably don't realise just how true that is! As a teenager the front man played football inside his parents' house and smashed their beloved collection of Star Trek plates! Dad Don and Mum Lynn are keen Trekkies and were gutted to lose their memorabilia…but just a few years later Theo actually bought them a new home from his bumper wage packet! Out of this world…

HORSEPLAY

Sylvan Ebanks-Blake could be called a thoroughbred striker—he was named after a racehorse!

The former Manchester United trainee, sold to Plymouth for £200,000, got his name because a friend of his father liked a bet at the races.

His dad bet on a horse called Sylvan's Delight, which won him a nice sum of money and helped determine the name of his newborn son who arrived in the world a few weeks later.

The striker, who later moved to Wolves and Ipswich, was also told by another betting man—former United boss Sir Alex Ferguson—that if he scored 100 goals in his first season away from Old Trafford he wanted the player back!

FACING THE FACTS

Turkey striker Tuncay earned a £4 million move out of the Premier League… thanks to Facebook!

The former Middlesbrough front man was desperate to leave left Stoke City and the Britannia Stadium, where he had played just 17 games in 18 months. He posted videos on his Facebook page of his personal top ten goals. And just days after the postings the former Fenerbahce man was on his way over the North Sea to join Wolfsburg.

STAR TURN

Midfielder Aaron Ramsey could have been playing with an oval ball instead of a round one.

The Wales star played local rugby while he was at school and even had the chance to join Super League side St Helens.

Luckily for his country and Arsenal supporters Ramsey, who was also a cross-country champion and 800-metre runner, decided football was his first love.

SMART SKIPPER

Former Sunderland skipper Lorik Cana is a history buff! The Albania star and ex-Marseille player is a brainbox and spoke French, German, Italian and before getting to grips with English. During his spare time in England he studied Balkan history, checked out the past of historic Durham Cathedral and walked along Hadrian's Wall!

GETTING SHIRTY

Wales star Craig Bellamy admits that one of his biggest heroes is…former teammate Carlos Tevez. The fiery striker even had the Argentina star's No.11 international shirt hanging in his home and revealed he just loves watching his Man City teammate play.

'He knows all about the shirt', admitted Bellars.

NOT SO TRIVIAL

Clarke Carlisle proved himself to be Britain's brainiest soccer player when he appeared on a TV programme in 2002. But even though he has five grade A and five grade As in his GCSEs, the former Burnley defender reckons his general knowledge is not so good now that he doesn't play Trivial Pursuit.

LESS VROOM…

England and Liverpool captain Steven Gerrard sold his 190 mph Aston Martin because he reckoned it was a bit too quick for him and he's 'not the best driver in the world'. Stevie G still has other cars that included another Aston, Ferrari, Bentley, Porsche and Mercedes!

QUICK-KICKS

- Defender Zat Knight is followed by his family wherever he goes! The former Fulham and then Bolton centre-half has his granddad George's name tattooed on his right shoulder and on his left shoulder is a tattoo dedicated to son Kai.
- Midfielder Michael Brown reckoned he could keep playing until he was 40 thanks to a bit of a racket! The former Sheffield United player started to play squash a few times every week against his mates during his time at Wigan because he believed it would boost his fitness levels and keep him sharp.
- Carlos Tevez stunned Manchester City's backroom staff when he bought each of them a 42-inch plasma TV as a thank you for their work at the end of season 2009–10.

NEVER STUMPED

England all-rounder James Milner is great at virtually every sport he takes part in.

Once the day job is over Milner would love nothing better than to keep on going in another sport…

'I'd love to play cricket in the summer. I have been tempted but I can't. I don't think the boss would be too happy if I got injured. I love my cricket and still watch', admitted Milner who has played in defence, midfield and even as a striker.

PLAYING THE BLUES

Their club is nicknamed the Blues and two Manchester City players took that quite literally by buying classy guitars! Defender Vincent Kompany and former midfielder Patrick Vieira both bought rock axes.

Kompany forked out £6,000 for a Gibson autographed by Oasis star Noel Gallagher, a big City fan. Frenchman Vieira paid £2,200 for a guitar signed by the group Texas.

STUCK FOR CHOICE

Joel Campbell was so proud of his impending call-up for the 2014 World Cup finals in Brazil that he dashed out to buy specially printed stickers. Forward Campbell, on loan from Arsenal to Greek side Olympiacos, bought 100 packets, a total of 500 stickers, and ripped open all of the packaging but failed to find a single image of himself.

The manufacturers confirmed that the Costa Rica striker was one of the 640 players who featured on the stickers.

NOT SO UNITED!

What have Robin van Persie, Phil Neville and Darren Fletcher got in common… besides the fact they all played for Manchester United? Unbelievably, all three of the Old Trafford stars allowed their sons to join the academy at… Manchester City!

Neville, who ended his career at Everton, allowed his boy to join City during his time at Goodison Park.

NO BULL

Batman was hit with a hefty fine when he was spotted taking part in a bull-run.

But it wasn't the caped crusader who was hit in the pocket but Real Madrid midfielder Asier Illarramendi. His manager Carlo Ancelotti spotted pictures of the player, dressed in the superhero's outfit, taking part in the dangerous dash with the bull.

FOWL PLAY

Joe Allen could have called 'fowl' when his fiancé bought him a surprise birthday present.

The Liverpool midfielder's other half presented him with a cockerel for his 24th birthday.

But the Wales star wasn't downhearted at getting the bird—he already had four hens!

QUICK SHOTS

- Defender Patrice Evra bought midfielder Park Ji-sung a red Ferrari when they both played at Manchester United. But it was only a toy! The Frenchman had promised to buy the South Korean a car for setting up a goal for him, and it was meant to replace one that Park had crashed on ice.
- Lanky England striker Peter Crouch reportedly forked out £3,000 for a karaoke machine so that he could try to out-sing some of his footballing mates.
- Rickie Lambert played through all the English lower leagues until he reached the Premier with Southampton. But the striker scored at Liverpool when he was just ten years old! Lambert was playing in a local cup final for Kirkby Boys but his side lost 3-2, as he scored at the Anfield Road end.
- Former Latvia keeper Aleksandrs Kolinko broke down in hysterics while on the bench at Crystal Palace, laughing at his side's own goal. He got a wake up

call when manager Trevor Francis slapped him in the face! The boss was fined £1,000 and the player left the club the following summer.

- Belgium striker Romelu Lukaku avoided injury when a wheel spun off his car on his way to a game. Everton, where he was on loan at the time, sent a car to pick him up from the scene of the accident and he went on to score the winner against West Ham.

TOP TRIVIA

LAST POST

Fans often sing 'Dodgy Keeper' when the man between the sticks is a bit suspect. But they would have been totally correct to sing their ditty during a First Division game in Sweden.

Shot-stopper Kim Christensen was caught kicking his posts closer together. When the ref spotted what he had done, he put the uprights back in their proper place.

The Swedish FA had a word with the player.

COLD COLE

Former England striker Carlton Cole admits he's not very good when it comes to clock watching.

"My time keeping is not good," he revealed. 'It's true. I once turned up for a game at halftime.'

When he was with West Ham he learnt that being called up to the national squad when Fabio Capello was in charge meant he had to keep an eye on his watch. 'He wouldn't stand for it and will embarrass you in front of your teammates if you are not early.'

SLEEP SUCKER

Wayne Rooney often looks very relaxed on the pitch and cool as a cucumber despite being watched by thousands of fans.

But the England and Manchester United striker has revealed that he often struggles to sleep without a light switched on or the TV flickering in the background. Sometimes he's even had a vacuum cleaner or hairdryer turned on to help him switch-off.

BALES OF SPORT

There was no escaping sport in the home of Gareth Bale, the world's most expensive footballer.

The Wales and Real Madrid star's dad, Frank, played amateur football.

Gareth's mum, Debbie, loved netball and hockey and his Uncle Chris turned out for a number of football clubs, including home town side Cardiff City.

CATNAP

Keeper Richard Kingson was nicknamed The Cat – but unlike other top shot-stoppers he did not earn that moniker through his agility. His teammates, during the player's time at Blackpool, reckoned the Ghana international is just like a four-legged feline and can sleep anywhere. They reckon he even went to sleep playing in a poker event!

JACK'S THE LAD

Striker Jack Midson borrowed a pair of boots from a teammate and scored a hat trick! After being out on loan, he returned to Oxford United to make his first appearance for almost four months and took the footwear from centre half Harry Worley as his own boots' studs were not long enough for the wet pitch. It was his first treble as a professional and his final goal earned a 4-3 victory at Torquay.

DO I KNOW YOU?

International darts ace James Wade thought he was about to be plagued by a troublesome fan during a shopping trip.

'I was in the local chemist and this guy went to me, "All right, Wadey?" I thought it was someone trying to be a pest. So, I replied, "All right",'said Wade, a double Grand Prix winner. Wade's other half at the time, TV presenter Helen Chamberlain, then got a text from the 'pest' asking how rude was her boyfriend?

Wade had only cold-shouldered one of his neighbours – England and Chelsea defender John Terry, a massive darts fan!

GRASSED UP

The ultimate fan of Manchester United will need to save up plenty of cash if they fancy a limited edition watch that contains grass from the Old Trafford pitch!

When they first went on sale in 2011 prices for the watches started at a staggering £31,400, more than the average man earned in a year!

The King Power Red Devil watch was produced by Hublot, the club's official timekeeper and used blades of grass from the Theatre of Dreams' turf that were picked specially by the club's groundsmen.

The grass was preserved, freeze-dried and inserted into the indexes, where they were coated with a special transparent lacquer.

Just 500 watches to a top price of £47,000 were produced and were expected to increase in value.

CHAPTER 5

THE CRAZY WORLD OF FOOTBALL

POSTPONED

Bad weather often leads to the postponement of games—but sometimes there are stranger reasons!

SNOW GO

Next time rain, snow or some other reason causes the postponement of your favourite team's game spare a thought for the fans of Inverness Thistle and Falkirk. In winter 1979, as freezing conditions gripped Scotland, the Scottish Cup second round game between these two sides was called off a staggering 29 times! It was due to be played on 8 January but it was 47 days later, on February 22, that the teams were finally able to face each other at Thistle's Kingsmills Park.

Inverness—who became Caledonian Thistle in 1994—probably wished the game hadn't gone ahead as they were thumped 4-0.

Falkirk would have been pleased with the result but just three days after that tie they had to play their delayed third round fixture against Dundee in which they were beaten by a late penalty.

FROZEN OUT

Back in winter 1963 snow and ice called a halt to more than 400 league and cup games in Scotland and England, which meant that the season in both countries had to be extended by a month.

The 'Big Freeze' saw Coventry City's FA Cup third round tie in January postponed and they eventually faced Lincoln City on the 16th time the fixture was rearranged.

Meanwhile, from 8 December to 16 February, Bolton Wanderers were unable to play a single competitive fixture.

On 16 March a complete football programme was played for the first time since early January.

NOT WORTH THE WAIT!

High-flying Everton were all set for their crucial match against Tottenham at White Hart Lane when a heavy snowfall caused a later postponement on Saturday, 29 November 1969.

The Division One game was rearranged for the evening of Wednesday, 17 December, and was 30 minutes old when a floodlight failure stopped play. The next available date was Wednesday, January 7, but Tottenham were then involved in an FA Cup replay and once again the game had to be called off. Eventually the match went ahead on Wednesday, March 11 and Tottenham lost 1-0. Just three days later Spurs had to go to Merseyside to face Everton in the return Division One fixture. They lost that game too and Everton went on to win the league title.

RELEGATION SICKNESS

Middlesbrough decided that with 23 players injured, ill or suspended they simply couldn't play their Premier League game at Blackburn in December 1996. So, the day before the game was due to go ahead they decided to call it off, but without permission from the league. The league held an inquiry and Blackburn said they wanted the points awarded to them. Officials said the game should be played but fined Boro £50,000 and deducted three points from them.

The game ended in a draw—but those three deducted points were the deciding factor that saw Middlesbrough relegated at the end of the season. Their woes did not stop there. Boro were also beaten in the finals of the FA and league cups that season.

DARK DAYS

Three English Premier league games were abandoned in a short period of time due to mystery floodlight failures. First the lights went out at Derby's new Pride Park when they faced Wimbledon in the first league match at the ground in August 1997. Referee Uriah Rennie called the game off eleven minutes into the second half after a squad of electricians couldn't work out why two generators had failed.

In November, players were thrown into darkness during the televised game between West Ham and Crystal Palace at Upton Park. Referee David Elleray abandoned the game after electricians couldn't find the fault.

The following month Selhurst Park was plunged into darkness when Wimbledon hosted Arsenal.

Electricians did get the lights back on for a time but they failed again and official Dermot Gallagher had to pull the plug on the game.

Two years later a police investigation into an attempt to sabotage the floodlights at a Charlton v Liverpool fixture with a remote control revealed why lights had failed previously. Detectives worked out that a Malaysian betting syndicate was behind the failures at West Ham and Selhurst Park. Four men later appeared in court and were sent to prison.

Police could find no proof of why the Derby lights failed.

WHY US? SOME STRANGE CANCELLATIONS...

- High winds in 2004 caused the cancellation of a number of English League matches. Wimbledon's game at Burnley was cancelled after the club revealed a 16-stone fan had nearly been blown over in the stands.

- An unexploded World War II bomb discovered near Sheffield United's Bramall Lane ground saw their Division Two game against Oldham called off in February 1985.

- Across the city at Hillsborough, Sheffield Wednesday's stadium, the Christmas game in 2010 was postponed because of frozen and burst pipes, which meant the toilets and cafes couldn't open.

- The Torquay v Portsmouth League Cup tie due at Plainmoor on Wednesday, 11 August 1999 was postponed because of a total eclipse of the sun! Police asked for the delay because they couldn't deal with the game and increased visitors to the area to see the eclipse.

- A sewer under Anfield's legendary Kop collapsed, which meant Liverpool had to postpone their first three home matches of 1987–88.

- In Scotland, in 1979, Airdrie and Stranraer set a British record of 29 postponements before Airdrie finally won the game 3-0.

STRANGE FACTS ABOUT... ROMAN PAVYLYUCHENKO

Roman Pavylyuchenko cost Tottenham £14 million when they signed him from Spartak Moscow in September 2008. The tall Russia striker arrived with a bit of history...and left London with even more!

- Before arriving in the Premier League, Roman insisted to his friends that there was no chance of him moving to England. His wife Larisa changed his mind...
- In fact it was just as well his other half was there for him because the player, sometimes called Super Pav by Spurs fans, admitted: 'I was useless at school. I just can't learn anything. Studying was always hard for me. My wife was quite good at English, but me?'
- History wasn't one of his strong points and he wasn't even sure about landmarks such as Big Ben and the River Thames when he arrived in London! He also confessed: 'You drive on the other side of the road. It took me time to adapt.'
- Before joining Spurs he had insisted: 'They are a club with great tradition. But since they are not playing in the Champions League we are more likely to reject their offer. If I go to England, I would want to play for Arsenal or Chelsea.'
- He was once handed a four-game ban for punching an opposition player.
- His mother Lyubov claimed: 'I know my son, and a glass of beer once a year

is all he allows himself. I've never seen him drunk.' But Pav confessed: 'After a game against Slovan I had so much to drink I got lost. The other players had to come looking for me.'

- His mum also dropped Pav in the mire when she revealed: 'He didn't want to go to England or leave Russia.'

- The player also had problems with a few drinks on the eve of his wedding when he admitted to almost falling off a hotel balcony. He also revealed he nearly repeated the balcony escapade when daughter Kristina was born.

- When he arrived at Spurs, the player claimed that his biggest challenge would be to learn English—and he began four and a half hours of lessons every week. 'My teammates are not teaching me any swear words but when I pick up some English and I try to use it on the pitch, they correct me if I am making mistakes', he said.

- When Tottenham manager Harry Redknapp substituted him against Manchester City, Pav stormed off, refused to join his teammates on the subs' bench and went straight to the dressing room.and then

- Pav departed from Tottenham in January 2012 after 113 games and 42 goals. He was sold to Lokomotiv Moscow for £8 million after claiming he would refuse to leave London that summer if Spurs didn't sell him during the January transfer window. He planned to sit out his contract until he could leave the club for nothing.

- He had not started a Premier League game in 2011–12 and there were reports—later denied by his agent—that he had been involved in a training ground bust-up with Spurs No.2 Kevin Bond. There were also suggestions he'd had a big disagreement with boss Harry Redknapp.

MARCUS HAHNEMAN: HARD-ROCKING KEEPER

Most goalkeepers are classed as eccentric but American shot-stopper Marcus Hahnemann would love it if you called him a real head-banger! The former Fulham, Reading, Wolves and Everton goalie is a massive hard rock music fan. In fact, the heavier the music the better!

Mind you, he's a guy also noted for his love of big guns and souped up cars! Although Wolves fans could also have spotted him riding to training in a pick-up truck or on his pedal cycle!

Hahnemann was ever-present during Reading's two-year stay in the Premier League, and played all of their 76 games.

Hahneman showed nerves of steel as he appeared in front of millions of fans as games were beamed live across the world by television. But behind closed doors in front of just a handful of people he wasn't so happy when he was given the chance to join thrash metal band Malefice for a recording session.

'I was more nervous going into the studio than going on the pitch for a game, I will tell you that right now', admitted Hahnemann.

'I thought "this is going to be awesome". Then the next email added that Dale [Butler, vocalist] would love to do some lyrics with a Premier League goalkeeper and I went "oh gosh, what have I got myself into?"'

'I am known for my heavy stuff, before a game or for training. That's the great thing about music, you can put on something heavy and get yourself going. My favourite band of all time is Tool. I have seen them four or five times and they have everything, pretty heavy—then I have seen Slipknot a few times and I love them. I have some Snow Patrol and other stuff. I got Jack Johnson…when I listen to that I am sitting around the fire, on the beach, that's what is great about music.'

Laid back Hahnemann does have a problem with another sport that is loved by his two sons—cricket!

'Hey you can't explain to an American that you can play a game for five days and not get a result. You can't even go there!'

FACT FILE

Marcus Stephen Hahnemann

Position: Keeper

Birth date: 15 June 1972

Birth place: Iowa, USA

Clubs: Seattle Sounders (twice), Colorado Rapids, Fulham, Rochdale (loan), Reading, Wolves, Everton

International: USA (9 caps, 0 goals)

STEPHEN IRELAND: HIS WORLD

Flash or eccentric—Stephen Ireland has certainly made football fans talk and smile about some of his antics. But when he splashed out £100,000 on a fish tank they did think fins couldn't get any worse! Here are just some of the more unusual aspects from Ireland's colourful world.

- The 6,000-litre fish tank, with mahogany and leather housing, was home to 500 exotic tropical fish and had pride of place in the snooker room at his mansion.
- 'It's a breathtaking tank. When people come to the door and see the tank, their

first reaction is "wow". There's a lot more to it than just glass and water. It's very complicated with the pumps and water system we have', explained Ireland.

- Ireland missed a Republic of Ireland game against the Czech Republic, claiming he had to visit his lonely girlfriend in the Emerald Isle.

- Then he told his Manchester City manager, Sven-Goran Eriksson that his granny had died and he was too upset to play. But his granny, Patricia Tallon was rather shocked when she read about her death in newspapers!

- Ireland then claimed it was his other gran, Brenda Kitchener, who had died. She too was surprised to read about her demise…. The player then said it was actually the elderly partner of one of his divorced grandfathers who had passed away. But then he came clean…

- He admitted: 'I decided at that stage that I must tell the truth and admit I had told lies. I realise that it was a massive mistake to say my grandmothers had died and I deeply regret it. It was wrong and I sincerely apologise as I have caused a lot of problems for many people. I would like to apologise to my grandmothers and all my family.'

- Ireland forked out £250,00 to buy his girlfriend Jessica Lawlor a Bentley for her birthday.

- It was painted red and white, had hearts and love messages embroidered into the leather seats and changed the Bentley 'B' to 'JL', her initials.

- The black Range Rover he bought was fine—but it didn't quite go with the pink alloy wheels!

- Then there was the Audi—in Manchester United red when he played in blue for Manchester City. He had it re-sprayed white. No one is sure what happened to the Superman petrol cap.

- Ireland also reckoned he was up for a fight—a cage fight! The midfielder even had a crack at the sport with a gruelling training regime that included kickboxing.

FACT FILE

Stephen James Ireland

Position: Midfielder

Birth date: 22 August 1986

Birth place: Cork, Ireland

Clubs: Manchester City, Aston Villa, Newcastle United (loan), Stoke City

International: Republic of Ireland (6 caps, 4 goals)

ZLATAN IBRAHIMOVIC: FLAWED GENIUS

Zlatan Ibrahimovic's transfers between some of Europe's top clubs have made him the most expensive player of all-time.

The total value of his transfers hit a staggering £134 million when he joined Paris Saint Germain in 2012. And his pay packets have also been stuffed to bursting point with claims that at one stage he was the world's best-paid player. It's no surprise that Ibrahimovic has been handed loads of money to show off his football skills as he's helped most of his teams win titles and trophies.

But the eight-times Swedish Footballer of the Year has also managed to thrust himself into the limelight for the wrong reasons.

Dutch giants Ajax sold Ibrahimovic shortly after he had clashed with club teammate Rafael van der Vaart during an international against Holland. The Dutchman claimed the Swede had intentionally hurt him. The Swede was with Juventus when the side were stripped of two Serie A titles and relegated following a game-rigging scandal.

Rather than play in a lower division, Ibrahimovic moved to Inter Milan where his success resulted in a transfer to Barcelona on a five-year contract in July 2009. But just over a year later he had fallen out with coach Pep Guardiola and was on his way back to Italy with AC Milan.

He was banned after punching Bari defender Marco Rossi in the stomach and then got another three game suspension for swearing at an assistant—although Ibrahimovic claimed he had been talking to himself! The Swede was also red-carded for slapping Napoli's Salvatore Aronica in an off-the-ball incident. He was also photographed kicking teammates Antonio Cassano, Christian Wilhelmsson and Rodney Strasser during training.

A big money, big-payday move to Paris Saint-Germain went through in July 2012—and Ibrahimovic's first season in France produced PSG's first title for ten years, with the striker contributing 30 goals.

But he was also in trouble once again and got a two-match ban for kicking St. Étienne keeper Stéphane Ruffier in the chest.

He received a similar suspension for stamping on Valencia winger Andrés Guardado.

Ibrahimovic also sparked a row in his home country when he said female footballers should not be given the same rewards as their male counterparts.

'Give them a bicycle with my autograph and that will be enough', he said after some male players were handed cars as reward for their international careers.

FACT FILE

ZLATAN IBRAHIMOVIC

Position: Striker

Birth date: 3 October, 1981

Birth place: Malmo, Sweden

Clubs: Malmo, Ajax, Juventus, Inter Milan, Barcelona, AC Milan, Paris Saint Germain

International: Sweden (98 caps, 48 goals)

WHAT HE'S WON:

- AJAX: Eredivisie 2002, 2004, Dutch Cup 2002, Johan Cruyff Shield 2002
- JUVENTUS: Serie A 2005, 2006 (both titles stripped), Italian Supercup 2006, 2008
- INTER MILAN: Serie A 2007, 2008, 2009, Italian Supercup 2006, 2008
- BARCELONA: La Liga 2010, Spanish Supercup 2009, 2019, UEFA Super Cup 2009, Club World Cup 2009
- AC MILAN: Serie A 2011, Italian Supercup 2011
- PARIS SAINT-GERMAIN: Ligue 1 2013, 2014 Ligue Cup 2014, Champions Trophy 2013
-

MARIO BALOTELLI: FIREWORKS AND MADNESS

He cost Manchester City £24 million from Inter Milan in 2010 and striker Mario Balotelli certainly lived up to his big billing…but not just with goals! The club should have known the hit man would be involved in more than just big match dramas because he had a history of being …eccentric!

- Even before he arrived in Manchester, Balotelli got into hot water when he appeared on television wearing an AC Milan shirt—despite being on the books of rivals Inter.

- He and his younger brother Enoch were arrested when they were discovered walking through the grounds of a women's prison. Mario told Italian police he had been curious.

- Balotelli and a group of friends were pictured leaving a strip club in the late hours of Thursday night-Friday morning with his Man City side due to play on the Saturday. Even though the striker played and scored in the game the following day, he broke club rules that prohibit players from late-night activities 48 hours before a game and that landed him with the maximum fine possible, two weeks' wages.

- Mario and pals used kitchen rolling pins, borrowed from a curry house, to stage a mock sword fight during a night out.

- He caused more than just fireworks on the pitch. 'I live right in the centre of Manchester. One day my brother Giovanni was in the street and looked up and said to his girlfriend, "How nice they're doing fireworks". It was me shooting them off the ninth floor', said Mario.

- Sparks also flew when he decided to set off some fireworks in the bathroom of his home in the early hours of the morning. The fire brigade was called when a towel caught fire and the player ended up sleeping in a Manchester hotel for the night.

- He was in bother after allegedly throwing darts at youth team players.

Although he missed his target, Man City still fined him £100,000.

- Knowing he was up for a laugh his City teammates decided Mario was fair game to be a victim of their pranks. 'If I wear strange shoes they stick them to the ceiling of the dressing room with tape. The other day they placed a live lobster in my car. Did I jump?' he revealed.

- He was involved in reported fights with Man City teammates Micah Richards, Jerome Boateng, Vincent Kompany and Aleksandar Kolarov… and even manager Roberto Mancini.

- Balotelli reckons he is allergic to grass and failed to come out for the second half of a Man City Europa League match in Kiev where the temperature was minus 6°C.

- Also during a game against Dynamo Kiev he had great difficulty in pulling on his warm up bib. He needed a hand from a coach and the whole hilarious episode was captured by television cameras and has since become a hit on YouTube.

- His flash Maserati car was reportedly impounded on 27 occasions during his time in Manchester leading to total of £10,000 in fines. He also parked across City's training ground entrance and blocked out the staff.

- Sent out by his mum to buy an iron, mop and vacuum cleaner, Mario returned from the Manchester department store with a giant trampoline, toy car racing set and two Vespa scooters. His mother was not amused!

- When a young fan asked for Mario's autograph the player demanded to know why he wasn't at school. The lad said he had been bullied, so Balotelli drove the youngster to school and had a chat with the head teacher about how to sort the problem.

- After his side had slaughtered local rivals United 6-1, the striker drove around Manchester high-fiving anyone he saw sporting a City shirt.
- He turned out for Italy wearing the wrong kit! The side had just launched a new home kit but the striker came out for the second half of the game in the old shirt, claiming he didn't like the new one!

FACT FILE

Mario Balotelli

Birth date: 12 August 1990

Birthplace: Palermo, Italy

Position: Striker

Clubs: Lumezzane, Inter Milan, Manchester City, AC Milan

PAULO DI CANIO: THE LOVEABLE ECCENTRIC

Paolo Di Canio was the sort of player that fans love—eccentric and brilliant! He hit the headlines for his fantastic football skills and also for his often-bonkers behaviour.

The signs of his eccentricity were there from an early age and as a youngster growing up in a part of Rome dominated by Roma fans he decided to follow their rivals Lazio, who became his first professional side.

Rows with the managers at Juventus and AC Milan led to him to Scotland to play for Celtic. No surprise that he was involved in a number of rows there and once refused to join a pre-season tour to Holland. That decision led to his departure for Sheffield Wednesday and an incident for which he became infamous—the pushing of referee Paul Alcock during a home game against Arsenal.

Alcock fell to the floor and Di Canio was banned for 11 matches and fined £10,000—quite a sum in 1998.

Once again he was on the move, this time to West Ham where he became a cult hero, scored one of the best goals in Premier League history and won a number of awards, including the club's own Player of the Season.

And in 2001 he received plaudits for a fantastic act of fair play during a game against Everton.

Di Canio had the chance to score with opposition keeper Paul Gerrard on the deck injured. Instead he caught the ball so the shot-stopper could get attention. Di Canio received an award for his good sportsmanship.

He moved back to Italy with Lazio in 2004 but was once again in hot water when he gave fascist salutes to his adoring fans. Again he found himself out of a job.

In 2008 he hung up his boots, eventually returning to the game as manager of Swindon Town in England's League Two.

He was soon creating headlines again—and not always for the right reasons. Di Canio had a very public row with striker Leon Clarke, was sent to the stands for questioning a referee's decision and humiliated keeper Wes Foderingham by taking him off after just 21 minutes, blaming him for a goal. Fans reacted furiously to the shot-stopper being taken off but Di Canio replied by saying if they weren't happy with his decisions he would refund their season ticket money.

Di Canio took the Robins to promotion as champions at the end of his first year in charge and later worked with volunteers to clear snow from the pitch so a game could go ahead...and bought them all pizza!

He quit as boss because of financial problems at the club that had restricted his transfer desires. Just a few months later, in March 2013, he took over as Sunderland gaffer and saved the side from relegation, but the following season the Italian almost caused a riot with the rules he imposed on his players.

In fact, many stars of the Black Cats side were so infuriated by his regulations that they contacted their union, the Professional Footballers' Association. Di Canio had imposed numerous fines for things such as being late for training, avoiding phone calls from the club doctor and skipping autograph signing sessions.

He also banned his players from having tomato ketchup and mayonnaise on their food, drinking coffee or having ice in drinks. He even outlawed singing before games!

'I've said that from now on if someone comes inside with a mobile phone, even in their bag, I'll throw it in the North Sea. They're banned', added the strict gaffer.

'The players can't be treated just according to what Paolo thinks', PFA chief Gordon Taylor insisted at the time. 'There are rules and procedures that both he and the club need to adhere to. Yes, the players have come to us for representation.'

The outcry from the players eventually led to Di Canio being sacked, not helped by the fact the team had picked up just one point in their first five games of the new season.

FACT FILE

Paolo Di Canio

Position: Forward

Birth date: 9 July 1968

Birthplace: Rome

Player: Lazio, Ternana (loan), Juventus, Napoli, AC Milan, Celtic, Sheffield Wednesday, West Ham, Charlton, Lazio, Cisco Roma

International: Italy (Under-21, 9 caps, 2 goals)

Manager: Swindon Town, Sunderland

DID YOU HEAR?

Players and manager sometimes say things they might regret…if we can understand what they mean….

- 'I was asked to see the psychologist when I went to Lyon. I came out with my arm around him telling him not to worry. I was 30 with a mortgage, three kids, 400 league games and in a new country.' Yorkshireman Mick McCarthy forgot to add he also played for the Republic of Ireland!

- 'I don't understand them getting drunk. In Italy we prefer to go off with a woman. I tell my players it's better than drink.' Roberto Mancini obviously didn't know the term 'wine, women and song' during his time as Man City manager.

- 'We have a saying in Spanish which is 'white liquid in a bottle has to be milk. So white liquid in a bottle: milk. You will know who is to blame. If I see John the milkman in the Wirral, where I was living, with this bottle, I'd say, "it's milk, sure".' If you know what Rafa Benitez was on about during his time at Liverpool…send in your answers on a postcard.

- 'It's very flattering to be asked, to take on another mantle, another ermine cloak. But I don't know what it means. I'm flattered but there are no dancing girls after the match.' Wolves fan and Led Zeppelin frontman Robert Plant is out of tune about his role as vice president of the Molineux club.

- 'Benjani scored his first goal in 14 games and never again could I say to him that if he had ten shots as an executioner the prisoner would still be alive.' Gaffer Harry Redknapp reveals the not-so-hot shot during his time at Portsmouth.

- 'I always watch football in 3D. Normally on a Sunday I'm always so drunk from Saturday night that it all looks a bit wonky.' Former Chelsea and Wimbledon hardman Vinnie Jones isn't sure if it's the drink or his TV…

- 'Spending $96m on someone who can get injured or be in bad form isn't correct to me, especially during this period of financial uncertainty.' Christoph Metzelder wasn't entirely sure why Real Madrid paid out a world record £80m to make Cristiano Ronaldo his teammate. Maybe he does now…

- 'I've come to Notts County because the club has great ambitions to get in the Premier League and I believe that can be achieved. That is why I am here, to be part of the future.' Former England defender Sol Campbell changed his mind after just one game for the Meadow Lane side and departed….

- 'I had to phone Jayden's school to get permission for him to play and that's a new one for us.' Bournemouth boss Eddie Howe needed teacher's help so that he could name Jayden Stockley, 16, in his squad.

- 'We were like a young lady with a fur coat on and no knickers. I'm placing everyone on the transfer list.' Micky Adams wasn't amused when his Port Vale side crashed at Notts County.

- 'I wanted 99 but the FA said no. I asked if I could have 77, they said no. I chose 52 for a number of reasons. Every time I walked out in 26 it didn't feel right.' Niklas Bendtner played the numbers game when he tried to get the right figures for the back of his shirt. His form for the Arsenal never did add up!

CHAPTER 6

THE REFEREES

REF JUSTICE: SHOCKING DECISIONS

Match officials aren't always the most popular people at a football match. In fact, sometimes it's a dangerous profession being a man in black…or to challenge his authority!

OCTOBER 1984

A referee slapped a youth who interrupted a game and was later shot dead!

Jose Castro, 25, had argued with three youths who had strolled onto the pitch and slapped one of them when they refused to leave.The youth returned to the pitch at Montpellier, France, with a shotgun and shot the referee in the head.

JULY 1994

The most famous shooting of a footballer was that of Andrés Escobar, whose own-goal helped to put Colombia out of the 1994 World Cup finals.

The 27-year-old was shot dead in his hometown of Medellin. Three men in vehicles often used by local drugs and gambling mafia allegedly shouted 'thanks for the own-goal' after pumping 12 bullets into the player.

Colombia had surprisingly lost 2-1 to the USA and the losers' coach, Francisco Maturana, plus several players, reportedly received death threats BEFORE the game. Midfielder Gabriel Gomez refused to play in the match. There were reports of attempted bribery and match fixing too.

During the match, Escobar had stretched to cut out a cross but instead stabbed the ball past his own keeper for the opening goal.

The USA team went on to qualify for the last 16 of the tournament while Colombia, who had been fancied to do well , went home in disgrace, despite beating Switzerland 2-0 in their final group match.

Colombia had beaten South American rivals Argentina 5-0 during qualification. That result led to celebrations in Colombia in which many were killed.

In an unrelated incident another player and a referee have been shot dead in Medellin.

FEBRUARY 1999

In 1999, south African referee Lebogang Petrus Mokgethi, 34, shot and killed a player during a game between Hartbeesfontein Wallabies and Try Agains. Hartbeesfontein fans ran on to the pitch when Try Agains scored, their side having been 2-0 down.

In the confusion on the pitch olice said Wallabies' captain Isaac Mkhwetha, 20, left the field to get a knife. Mokgethi grabbed his pistol from a friend in the crowd.

Mkhwetha stabbed at Mokgethi who shot the player in the chest. He died shortly afterwards.

JULY 2004

In 2004 in South Africa's Eastern Cape, a referee shot dead a coach and then fled following a row over a yellow yard. The card was the catalyst for a mass protest led by Marcelle players. The referee drew a firearm and shot the Marcelle coach in the chest. The coach died on the pitch. Prior to that two players had been hit in the hand by stray bullets from his gun.

NOVEMBER 2011

A referee was shot dead during a game in Venezuela. The incident happened during a Futsal event in San Rafael Cordero. Futsal is a football variation played with a soft ball.

Timoleon Castillo was shot three times as players celebrated a goal. The referee's attacker fled during the confusion.

MAY 2013

A referee punched by a player during a game spent a week in a coma and then died.

Ricardo Portillo, 46, died in Salt Lake City, Utah. The referee had handed a yellow card to the 17-year-old player who then hit him on the side of the head.

Portillo had previously suffered broken ribs and a broken leg sustained in attacks during games.

'People don't know it's a game', said his daughter Johana Portillo. 'We're all there to have fun, not to go and kill each other.'

JULY 2013

In ancient times being hung, drawn and quartered was the fate that met many criminals but even that treatment sounds tame compared to what happened to referee Otavio Jordao da Silva de Catanhede.

He was beheaded and his head displayed on top of a wooden stake after a match in Brazil.

Jordao had been involved in a row with Josenir dos Santos Abreu, which resulted in the player being sent off. Instead he began to fight with the referee, who stabbed the player with a knife. The player died on his way to hospital. Friends and family of the player went onto the pitch, stoned the referee, quartered his body and then put his head on a stake in the middle of the pitch.

JANUARY 2014

A footballer was shot dead and one of his teammates injured when a gunman shot on them and two other players from the same team. All four of the players were in a hairdresser's when the gunman on a motorbike drove past and opened fire.

The Colombians all played for the Union Magdalena side and were visiting the city of Santa Marta. Ferley Reyes died and Luis Diaz Asprilla was taken to hospital with injuries. The two other players were not hurt.

Their team doctor reckoned they were just 'in the wrong place at the wrong time', as they knew no one in the city.

OI, REFEREE! AMAZING INCIDENTS

They may seem unreal but these stories involving the men in black really did happen

PHANTOM WHISTLER

One of the first rules of football is that you always play to the referee's whistle.

The Kuwait national side did that, only it wasn't the official's, and stopped when they heard a shrill whistle. France played on to score a goal and make it 4-1 in a 1982 World Cup game.

Sheikh Fahad Al-Ahmad Al-Sabah, Kuwait FA president, was so incensed that he rushed onto the pitch to argue with the man in black and said he would take his team off the pitch if the goal wasn't scrubbed. Amazingly, the referee decided to chalk off the goal.

France still went on to score a fourth goal and the official was later barred from international games.

Seeing red

Nineteen red cards in one game was the incredible total dished out by referee Jose Manuel Barro Escandon.

Incredibly, 18 of those sendings-off were handed out AFTER the players had left the pitch!

The ref had abandoned the Spanish regional league match barely ten minutes into the second half following a mass braw that occurred in response to the issue of the first red card.

The players had started to wade into each other after Recreativo Linense had a player sent off against Saladillo de Algeciras.

The ref went to the teams' changing rooms and dished out nine red cards to each side.

NO HELPING SOME PEOPLE

Trying to help out the referee didn't pay off for two top England players.

Paul 'Gazza' Gascoigne was playing for Glasgow Rangers against Hibs in 1995 when he saw the official drop a yellow card on the pitch.

Gazza, forever the joker, decided to yellow card Dougie Smith, the man in black – but the ref obviously lacked a sense of humour as he booked the midfielder for real!

And, back in 1977 Manchester City goalkeeper Joe Corrigan decided he would help out when the ref couldn't find the penalty spot during his side's clash with Derby County. Corrigan paced out the 12 yards to where the spot should be and the ref booked him!

ARE YOU WATCHING?

Match officials are quite often accused of being blind or needing a sight test. Those sentiments rang true during a 1993 Scottish Premier League game between Partick Thistle and Dundee United. United scored through Paddy Connolly but as the ball bounced back out of the goal it was caught by Thistle defender Martin Clark.

Clark handed the ball to his keeper, Andy Murdoch, who kicked it towards the centre circle for the game to restart.

Amazingly the ref and his assistant hadn't spotted that the ball had been over the goal line and just allowed play to continue.

Luckily Dundee still won the game without the aid of their goal that wasn't.

CHEERS...

Bemused fans couldn't believe some of the wayward tackles that the referee let players get away with in the Belarusian Premier League clash between Vitebsk and Naftan in 2008.

And they were stunned at how the official appeared to be staggering around the pitch and kept his yellow and red cards firmly in his pocket. At the end of the match the referee was helped from the pitch and taken to hospital.

Tests proved Sergei Shmolik, a ref with international credentials, had drunk vast amounts of alcohol. The Belarus FA later suspended the official who claimed he had problems with a bad back rather than beer.

SPOOKY!

Some footballers have amazing superstitions. Here are just a few of them...

COOL CUSTOMER

You might not be surprised to hear that superstar David Beckham insisted on having a brand new kit for every game in which he played. But what would you think about the former England captain having to make sure that his refrigerator was correctly stocked and arranged?

It's true! Becks would even rush out to the shops and buy another can of cola if there weren't the right number in his fridge.

WEIRD BUT TRUE

England's Phil Jones puts his feet first when it comes to match preparation. The Manchester United defender-midfielder puts his left sock on first for home matches and his right sock on first at away games!

'I just can't help it and know it is weird,' he admitted.

TOILING...

Joe Cole is in a league of his own when it comes to his ritual.

'I know superstitions mean nothing and it's all in your head really, but I've got so many it's not true,' said the Aston Villa, West Ham, Chelsea, Liverpool and former England midfielder.

'I never kick the ball in the changing room, I always use the same toilet before the game....'

But his lucky shin pads top the list: 'I won the league with Chelsea in them. I left them at home before the World Cup finals in Germany and I had to get them sent over.'

LAST MAN

Kolo Toure just HAS to be the last player out onto the pitch. He is so adamant about this that one game actually started without him on the turf! During his time with Chelsea, the Ivory Coast defender refused to go onto the pitch because teammate William Gallas was still receiving medical treatment after halftime.

To make matters worse, when Toure did get involved in the game he got a yellow card because he had forgotten to get the referee's permission to walk onto the grass.

PEED OFF

You wouldn't want to face keeper Sergio Goycochea in a penalty shootout. The Argentina shot-stopper had to relieve himself on the pitch before facing spot-kicks because he believed it brought him good luck.

It all started because he stuck to the laws of the game at the 1990 World Cup finals. Not being allowed to leave the pitch because the game was technically still in progress, Goycochea urinated. His team won and from then on he decided that peeing was the only way to go – and he would do it in the centre circle, masked by a ring formed by his teammates.

SLAP AND SPIT

Dutchman Johan Cruyff, one of the most skilled players the world has ever seen, always believed he had to rely on a few lucky charms before games. First he had to slap his own Ajax keeper Gert Bals in the stomach and then he had to spit out his chewing gum on the opposition's half of the pitch before the kick-off!

JAGGED EDGE

England and Everton defender Phil Jagielka is very superstitious!

He always eats chicken and pasta the night before a game and listens to the same music on the way to the ground!

BITERS, SPITTERS AND STAMPERS!

Football can be a hazardous game with many injuries ranging from a slight muscle pull to torn hamstrings, broken metatarsals and legs and even career ending knocks. But it's the unexpected that brings the shocks…stamping, spitting and even biting!

Few fans will argue against the praise Louis Suarez gets as an excellent forward who can turn matches with his goal-scoring skills.

But there have been some big question marks against his temperament.

Keepers have to ensure they can block his shots whilst a few players have also learnt you avoid his teeth! Many fans expected him to make a big name for himself at the 2014 World Cup finals in Brazil – but they hadn't expected it to be for BITING an opponent on the shoulder!

The incident, involving Italy defender Giorgi Chiellini, was missed by the referee but after using video evidence FIFA, world football's governing body, hit Suarez with a four-month ban. The striker was forbidden entry to stadia, was not allowed to train and outlawed from ANY football activity.

That did not stop Barcelona making a £75m move for the Liverpool forward who had already served a ten-game ban for sinking his gnashers into the arm of Chelsea defender Branislav Ivanovic. Although a referee also missed that incident in April 2013 the Football Association reviewed television footage and gave a retrospective ban. The player was also fined by his club.

Mind you, Suarez had past form… he was banned for eight games and fined £40,000 in 2011 for racially abusing Manchester United's France defender Patrice Evra. And in 2010 Suarez, whilst playing for Ajax of Amsterdam he was banned for seven matches for biting PSV Eindhoven's Otman Bakkal during a Dutch league game. And in 2011 he was banned for one game for making an offensive gesture to Fulham fans.

A former Liverpool player, El Hadji Diouf, earned a reputation that was both unwanted and unsavoury. The Senegal forward spat at a Celtic fan during a UEFA Cup game in Scotland. He was banned for two games and fined £60,000.

There were also numerous other allegations of spitting at fans, including an incident involving a young fan at Middlesbrough.

During his time at Bolton Wanderers he was fined for spitting on Portsmouth's

Arjan de Zeeuw – and his club sent him to see a psychologist.

Torquay midfielder Joss Labadie received a ten-game ban for biting an opponent when the incident was revealed on Twitter! The player denied the charge of an assault on Chesterfield's Ollie Banks during a 2014 League Two game. But the FA found him guilty and as well as the ban issued a £2,000 fine.

OUCH...

- Argentina striker Sergio Aguero was sent-off in 2008 for spitting at Bolton's Matt Taylor in a UEFA Cup game. Aguero, who at the time was playing for Atlético Madrid, had only been on the pitch as a sub for 12 minutes. He was banned for two games, later rescinded to one match.
- Sunday League footballer Mark Ward was jailed for four months in 2009 when he stamped on a player laying injured on the ground. A court found Ward, of Whale Hill team in northeast England, guilty of common assault.
- Fulham's German defender Sascha Riether was banned for three games in 2013 after stamping on Manchester United's Adnan Januzaj during a Premier League game. He became the first player to be punished by a new system where three former referees look at incidents on video that the match official has not spotted during the game.

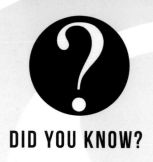

DID YOU KNOW?

- Ridgeway Rovers, where England winger Andros Townsend began playing football as a youth, has produced a string of other stars. They include Townsend's Tottenham teammate, striker Harry Kane, former England captain David Beckham and Arsenal hopeful Nico Yennaris.

- Midfielder Leon Britton began his Swansea City career in League Two and played through League One and the Championship with the club to reach the Premier League. He did leave them for Sheffield United in 2010, but was back to Wales within five months.

- Keeper Kelvin Davis, who joined Southampton from Sunderland in July 2006 for a transfer fee of around £2 million, was the first Saint to waive his wages for a few weeks when the club got into financial difficulties.

- Newcastle United fans were stunned when Argentina winger Jonas Gutierrez joined them in a queue at the city centre's Eldon Square shopping centre to buy a new Apple iPad3 on the day of its release.

- He's often referred to by his nickname of 'The Ox', but before his move to Arsenal, England midfielder Alex Oxlade-Chamberlain had always been called Chambo. The player admitted that during his time at Southampton he felt sorry for fans who initially had to pay out for replica shirts with Oxlade-Chamberlain on the back.

- England keeper Ben Foster worked as a chef before becoming a full-time footballer and reckons he can still 'knock anything up from a spaghetti Bolognese to a good stew.'

- Theo Walcott was the youngest player to score a hat trick for England. He was 19 when he hit three in a World Cup qualifier against Croatia in 2008.

- Jack Butland wears gloves on the pitch as one of England's most promising keepers but he also likes to watch boxing, and former World Champion Muhammad Ali is one of his all-time heroes.

- Manchester United and England midfielder Michael Carrick began his youth career with Wallsend Boys', the club that also produced a number of other top class players, including Premier League record scorer Alan Shearer, Lee Clark, Peter Beardsley and Steve Bruce.

- Defender Ryan Shawcross rejected an offer to play for Wales, where he was brought up. Stoke City's former Manchester United youngster said that he never had any intention of playing for the principality. He was able to play as a Wales schoolboy because he was educated in the country.

- Sergio Aguero, the 37th Argentine to play in the Premier League when he signed for Manchester City, loves to keep football memorabilia from the big games in which he has played. He's got his boots and shirt from City's final-day victory over QPR that clinched the Premier League title in 2012, but someone else—he doesn't know who—grabbed the match ball before he could nab it.

- Phil Neville reckons his longevity in the game was due to lots of sleep! 'It's a big part of my life. My kids put me to bed for hours in the afternoon', he smiled. Neville played in the English top tier from 1995–2013 with Manchester United and Everton and won 59 England caps.

CHAPTER 7

THE WORLD ACCORDING TO …

GORDON STRACHAN

As a player he was a battling midfielder. And what he lacked in height he more than made up for in skill and determination during his time at Aberdeen, Manchester United and Leeds United.

When Gordon Strachan moved into management he became an entertainer with his eccentric television interviews and fast retorts… but he wasn't the easiest person to interview. Here are some of his quick quips…

'I tried to get the disappointment out of my system by going for a walk. I ended up 17 miles from home and I had to phone my wife, Lesley, to come and pick me up.'

'When he [Claus Lundekvam, Southampton defender] was carried off at Leicester someone asked me if he was unconscious, but I didn't have a clue. He's always like that.'

'I've got more important things to think about. I've got a yogurt to finish by today, the expiry date is today. That can be my priority rather than Agustin Delgado'

[Southampton forward, Strach wasn't keen on]

'Scotland have a system which is getting better, but it's players who win and lose games. Look at England. They have a system, but if the opposition players jump higher, tackle harder and shoot better, your system is in trouble.'

'I can't even make myself anything to eat. I had to phone her [wife] and she said, "I've left something to put in the microwave". An hour later and I'm asking, "Where's the microwave?"'

'Pahars [Marian, Southampton forward] has also caught every virus going except a computer virus and he is probably working on that even now.'

ANY QUESTIONS?

Question: 'This might sound like a daft question, but you'll be happy to get your first win under your belt, won't you?'

Strachan: 'You're right. It is a daft question. I'm not even going to bother answering that one. It is a daft question, you're spot on there.'

Question: 'Gordon, can we have a quick word, please?'

Strachan: 'Velocity.'

Question: 'There goes your unbeaten run. Can you take it?'

Strachan: 'No, I'm just going to crumble like a wreck. I'll go home, become an alcoholic and maybe jump off a bridge. I think I can take it, yeah.'

Question: 'Gordon, you must be delighted with that result?'

Strachan: 'You're spot on! You can read me like a book!'

Question: 'You don't take losing lightly, do you Gordon?'

Strachan: 'I don't take stupid comments lightly either.'

Question: 'In what areas do you think Middlesbrough were better than you today?'

Strachan: 'What areas? Mainly that big green one out there...'

Question: 'Welcome to Southampton Football Club. Do you think you are the right man to turn things around?'

Strachan: 'No. I was asked if I thought I was the right man for the job and I said, "No", I think they should have got George Graham because I'm useless.'

Question: 'There's no negative vibes or negative feelings here?'

Strachan: 'Apart from yourself, we're all quite positive round here. I'm going to whack you over the head with a big stick, down negative man, down.'

FACT FILE

Gordon David Strachan

Birth place: Edinburgh

Birth date: 9 February 1957

Position: Midfielder

Player: Dundee, Aberdeen, Manchester United, Leeds United, Coventry City

Manager: Coventry City, Southampton, Celtic, Middlesbrough, Scotland

International: Scotland (50 caps, 5 goals)

IAN HOLLOWAY

A player who spent most of his career with home town club Bristol Rovers and Queens Park Rangers, Ian Holloway could probably best be described as decent and reliable rather than headline-hitting. But when he moved into management with Rovers, followed by stints elsewhere, he became a media favourite. Amusing, often brilliant and sometimes totally unreal, any interview with the man known as Ollie was guaranteed to entertain. These are some of his more famous – or infamous – quotes…

'We are like the Men in Black zapping the aliens together. Bosh! Zap!' On another planet during his time as Blackpool boss.

'I'm being serious when I say we've had thousands, not hundreds, of players recommended to us by agents. I feel like a gold prospector. One of them may be a lump of gold but most won't be.'

Searching for nuggets at Blackpool.

'We might as well go back to being cavemen, grab our girl by the hair, drag her into the cave whether she wants to come in or not because we may as well live in that age. We've come forward haven't we?'

And all because there was no goal-line technology.

'It's all very well having a great pianist playing but it's no good if you haven't got anyone to get the piano on the stage in the first place, otherwise the pianist would be standing there with no bloody piano to play.' Reaction to criticism after he was forced to play defenders in midfield.

'It was lucky that the linesman wasn't stood in front of me as I would have poked him with a stick to make sure he was awake.'

'Apparently it's my fault that the *Titanic* sank.' His reply to criticism from Plymouth fans.

'He's six foot something, fit as a flea, good looking – he's got to have something wrong with him. Hopefully he's hung like a hamster – that would make us all feel better. Having said that, me missus has got a pet hamster at home, and his cock's massive.' Ollie's take on Cristiano Ronaldo.

'You can say that strikers are very much like postmen: they have to get in and out as quick as they can before the dog starts to have a go.'

'To put it in gentleman's terms if you've been out for a night and you're looking for a young lady and you pull one, some weeks they're good looking and some weeks they're not the best. Our performance today would have been not the best looking bird but at least we got her in the taxi. She weren't the best looking lady we ended up taking home but she was very pleasant and very nice, so thanks very much, let's have a coffee.'

All that after an 'ugly' win at Chesterfield…and possibly his most famous reply…

'I have such bad luck at the moment that if I fell in a barrel of boobs I'd come out sucking my thumb.'

'Paul Furlong [striker] is my vintage Rolls Royce and he cost me nothing. We polish him, look after him, and I have him fine-tuned by my mechanics. We take good care of him because we have to drive him every day, not just save him for weddings."

'We need a big, ugly defender. If we had one of them we'd have dealt with [Notts] County's first goal by taking out the ball, the player and the first three rows of seats in the stands.'

'I don't see the problem with footballers taking their shirts off after scoring a goal. They enjoy it and the young ladies enjoy it too. I suppose that's one of the main reasons women come to football games, to see the young men take their shirts off. Of course they'd have to go and watch another game because my lads are as ugly as sin.'

HARRY REDKNAPP

Straight talking Harry Redknapp, father of former England midfielder Jamie and uncle to Frank Lampard, has been branded a 'wheeler dealer' of football transfers. But he's also proved that he can manage teams of many sizes having been in charge at Bournemouth, West Ham, Portsmouth, Tottenham and QPR. The former West Ham player was once linked to the England manager's job. He's also had some great things to say about our favourite game…

'Even when they had Moore, Hurst and Peters, West Ham's average finish was about 17th. It just shows how crap the other eight of us were.'

'Where are we in relation to Europe? Not too far from Dover.'

He didn't rate West Ham's UEFA Cup hopes too highly…

'I sorted out the team formation last night lying in bed with the wife. When your husband's as ugly as me, you'd only want to talk football in bed.'

'Before I signed Luther Blissett for Bournemouth, my chairman at the time said, "Harry, they tell me he's over the hill. Why are we signing him?" I said, "He'll score goals." In his first game he scored four against Hull. After the game the chairman said, "We haven't seen the best of him yet." I said, "I think we have."'

"I signed Marco Boogers off a video. He was a good player but a nutter. They didn't show that on the video.'

'The sad part is that the ones [players] who do well want to go, but you cannot move the ones who are useless.'

'You will never get a better chance to win a match than that. My missus could have scored that one.'

England striker Darren Bent got it in the ear during Harry's time at Tottenham…

'After shooting practise yesterday, I had to drive up the M27 and collect four balls.'

He wasn't impressed with Benjani's aim at Portsmouth!

'There are a lot of players at this club who earn far too much money. Far too much for their ability and what they give to the club... I don't really want to see the owners have their pants taken down like they have in the past.'

After his arrival at QPR.

'I've never wrote a letter in my life. I couldn't write a letter, I write like a two-year-old and I can't spell. You talk to anybody at the football club, I don't write. I couldn't even fill a team sheet in.'

'He felt he was too good to be on the substitute's bench. I've fined him two weeks' wages, which is £130,000, which isn't bad for two weeks work is it? How do I handle a player like that? Maybe he'll find out in January.'

Portugal defender José Bosingwa stayed at QPR the following January…but was allowed to leave the following summer.

'This is a football club that has been put together by I don't know who, and I don't know how. It's a mish-mash of players with people playing where they want to play. It's scary.'

His view of Tottenham in 2009.

FACT FILE

Henry James Redknapp

Birth place: Poplar, East London

Birth date: 2 March 1947

Position: Midfielder

Player: West Ham United, Bournemouth, Brentford, Seattle Sounders, Bournemouth

Manager: Bournemouth, West Ham United, Portsmouth, Southampton, Portsmouth, Tottenham, QPR

JOSÉ MOURINHO

When he arrived for his first stint at Chelsea manager Jose Mourinho labelled himself as 'The Special One.' He had every right to the name, having already won two Portuguese league titles, a Champions League and UEFA Cup with Porto. And the Portugal-born boss lived up to his own statement by guiding the Blues to two Premier League titles, an FA Cup and two League Cups before moves to Inter Milan and Real Madrid—where he was among the trophies again with both clubs—before a return to Chelsea in 2013.

He seldom lets fans or reporters down with his pre and post-match press conferences…

'It's like having a blanket that is too small for the bed. You pull the blanket up to keep your chest warm and your feet stick out. I cannot buy a bigger blanket because the supermarket is closed. But the blanket is made of cashmere.'

…and all because Chelsea had an injury crisis!

'If I wanted to have an easy job I would have stayed at Porto. Beautiful blue chair, the UEFA Champions League trophy, God, and after God, me.'

BC…before Chelsea job

'Omelettes, eggs. No eggs, no omelettes. And it depends on the quality of the eggs in the supermarket. They are class one, two or three and some are more expensive than others and some give you better omelettes. When the class one eggs are not available you have a problem.'

Why was he talking about eggs? It's about transfer funds. Honest!

'My history as a manager cannot be compared with Frank Rijkaard's history. He has zero trophies and I have a lot of them.'

He was not the biggest fan of former Barcelona boss Rijkaard…

'I am coach of Real but Barca doesn't worry me. My only concern is to grow Real. Barca are great rivals and we respect them. If I am hated at Barcelona, it is their problem but not mine. Fear is not a word in my football dictionary.'

When he took over at Real Madrid.

'What position is my wife in? Eighth, at least.'

After hearing a survey named him ninth most influential person in the world

'Look, I'm a coach. I'm not Harry Potter. He is magical, but in reality there is no magic. Magic is fiction and football is real.'

But José is still wizard in Chelsea fans' eyes.

'There are only two ways for me to leave Chelsea. One way is in June 2010 when I finish my contract and if the club doesn't give me a new one. It is the end of my contract and I am out. The second way is for Chelsea to sack me. The way of the manager leaving the club by deciding to walk away, no chance! I will never do this to Chelsea supporters.'

He had a bust up with owner Roman Abramovich…but then made up and returned!

'Look, we're not entertaining? I don't care; we win.'

On his Chelsea side of 2006-07.

'Pressure? There is no pressure. Bird Flu is pressure. (The Press laughed) No, you laugh, but I am being serious. I am more worried about the swan than I am about football.'

'I am not concerned about how Chelsea are viewed morally. What does concern me is that we are treated in a different way to other clubs. Some clubs are treated as devils, some are treated as angels. I don't think we are so ugly that we should be seen as the devil and I don't think Arsene Wenger [Arsenal manager] and David Dein [Arsenal chairman] are so beautiful that they should be viewed as angels.'

Ouch!

'Everybody was waiting for Chelsea not to win every game and one day, when we lose, there will be a holiday in the country. But we are ready for that.'

'We have eight matches and eight victories, with 16 goals, but people say we cannot play, that we are a group of clowns. This is not right.'

The Chelsea circus?

'As we say in Portugal, they brought the bus and they left the bus in front of the goal. I would have been frustrated if I had been a supporter who paid £50 to watch this game because Spurs came to defend. There was only one team looking to win, they only came not to concede – it's not fair for the football we played.'

After a goalless draw against London rivals Tottenham

'This is nothing against Sir Alex [Ferguson, Man United manager] whatsoever. After the game on Wednesday we were together in my office and we spoke and drank wine. Unfortunately it was a very bad bottle of wine and he was complaining, so when we go to Old Trafford for the second leg, on my birthday, I will take a beautiful bottle of Portuguese wine.'

FACT FILE

José Mario dos Santos Mourinho Félix

Birth place: Setubal, Portugal

Birth date: 26 January 1963

Position: Midfielder

Player: Rio Ave, Belenenses, Sesimbra, Comércio e Industria

Manager: Benfica, Uniao de Leiria, Porto, Chelsea, Inter Milan, Real Madrid, Chelsea

MICK MCCARTHY

There are managers who are dream interviewees, never short of a word or five, know how to slip in a bit of humour and can be brutally honest about what they think.

Say hello to one of them, Yorkshire-born Mick McCarthy who was a stalwart defender for a number of league clubs and the Republic of Ireland before moving into management.

'I'm bitter, twisted, sore, narked and upset. Things like that knock the stuffing out of you.'

He doesn't like bad decisions!

'My mother told me there would be days like these. She didn't tell me when and she didn't tell me how many.'

If it wasn't for bad luck, he'd have no luck at all…

'I don't want a load of psychologists on my phone on Monday morning, let me tell you, because that's what I'll be getting. 'We will help you deal with the rigours of the Premiership and give them mental stability' and all that.'

He can cope with defeat on his own, thank you very much!

'Anyone who uses the word "quintessentially" in a halftime talk is talking crap.'

A believer in staight talk.

'We are not going to roll over on our bellies, get tickled, and say, "Isn't it great we're in the Premiership?"'

His Wolves side did put up a fight as they lost 2-0 at Chelsea.

'Playing with some of the best around was great and I learned a lot from it. I learned that I am far worse than I thought I was!'

Forget football, Mick had just won a golf event that included top golfer Padraig Harrington.

'Of course, he couldn't tell me afterwards, "I've lost my voice", because he couldn't speak.'

Keeper Kelvin Davis lost his voice and got stick for not being vocal enough…

'Walking around, showing your disappointment and being a sour puss is not the way forward.'

Always think on the bright side of life.

'Some people might be frustrated with that result? Some people can f**k off.'

Reacting to suggestions that fans might not be happy with Ipswich's 1-1 draw at

Leeds.

'At the moment we've got 16 first team players. My initials stand for Mick McCarthy, not Merlin the Magician.'

'That Serbian keeper is a big tart doing that because there's nothing wrong with him.'

During commentary for the BBC at the 2010 World Cup when the keeper went down injured.

'No, and I asked all the lads to go out there and knock seven bells out of everybody as well like I normally do. Shame that isn't it? They went out there and played free-flowing football and were rampant for 45 minutes. What were they playing at?'

After a journalist pointed out his side had picked up no cautions during a game.

FACT FILE

Michael Joseph McCarthy

Position: Defender

Birth place: Barnsley, Yorkshire

Birth date: 7 February 1959

Player: Barnsley, Manchester City, Celtic, Lyon, Millwall

Manager: Millwall, Republic of Ireland, Sunderland, Wolves, Ipswich Town

International: Republic of Ireland (57 caps, 2 goals)

TOP TRIVIA

YOU'RE NICKED!

A football fan on the run from police for five years was arrested when he couldn't resist watching his favourite team. Tiecoura Bakayoko fled to France when he was due to stand trial in Kent, England, for allegedly having fake identification documents. But when Paris Saint Germain were drawn to play at Chelsea in the Champions League he just had to see the game.

Police, who had been looking for him since he skipped bail in 2009 nabbed him when he landed at Heathrow shortly before the game in 2014.

PSG lost 2-0 in the quarter-final tie!

SING FOR YOUR SUPPER

The British Government spent £21,000 to find a new terrace chant – something that many fans create for free every weekend!

Supporters are legendary for coming up with new football chants, often based on the latest news and sports headlines from the past few days or hours.

Yet ministers handed out a fortune to get fans to come up with new songs believing that it would increase literacy skills!

The winning song was by fan Terry Cook, an ode to a veteran Southend striker: "Underground, overground, signed on a free, he's Dougie Freedman of SUFC."

It was sung to the Wombles song!

NICE PLACES

A poll of fans made Old Trafford the friendliest football stadium in England – with Millwall's New Den the unfriendliest.

Man United's Theatre of Dreams got the nod ahead of Arsenal's Emirates Stadium, Liverpool's Anfield, Chelsea's Stamford Bridge and St. James' Park, Newcastle.

Millwall were ahead of Elland Road, Leeds; Upton Park, West Ham; Ninian Park, Cardiff (although they now have a new ground); and St. Andrews, Birmingham City.

BACK OF THE NET!

Strikers who hit a lean spell should take note of amateur player John O'Brien who had scored for his club in every decade since the 1950s!

But as the clock ticked toward 2000 and another new decade he was worried he wasn't going to hit the back of the net in the Noughties.

John decided to get his wife to place a bet with the bookies that he would grab a goal before 2010. And he did! John, from Ewell, Surrey, got bookies to accept a bet of £20 at odds of 25/1, that he would grab the vital goal. And when he lined up for Old Salesians Veterans against National Physical Laboratories, playing in a back four, he tapped home from close range and his wife picked up £500. John donated the cash to his club.

CHAPTER 8

STRANGE BUT TRUE!

BET THAT HURT!

Injuries are part and parcel of playing football. But some stars have been ruled out of games by accidents that left them red-faced…

SILLY SERGIO

Argentina striker Sergio Aguero was a vital part of the Manchester City side chasing its first Premier League title.

But he was ruled out of action by an injury described by his then boss Roberto Mancini as "stupid".

No official explanation was given but favourite causes were that he was riding his three-year-old youngster's bike or that he fell off the team coach.

SALAD DAYS

Dave Beasant made history when he became the first keeper to save an FA Cup Final penalty in Wimbledon's historic victory over Liverpool in 1989.

He also earned a place in the history books when he was ruled out of action for a number of games after dropping a jar of salad cream on his foot!

KNOCKOUT GOAL

Winger Perry Groves was famed for warming Arsenal's bench between 1986 and 1992.

But he got so excited watching one game from the subs' seats that he jumped up when the Gunners scored, hit his head on the dugout roof and knocked himself out cold.

DIFFICULT DRILLS

When former England striker Darius Vassell discovered a large blood blister under his big toenail he decided he didn't need to seek medical help.

The Aston Villa hitman picked up a power drill to bore through the nail but also picked up an infection that ruled him out of the next game.

BAD ADVERT

Shaun Goater became a goal-scoring legend during his days with Manchester City.

But it was a goal by teammate Nicolas Anelka against Birmingham City that he will never forget!

Goater joined Anelka to celebrate the strike, kicked an advertising board and had to be substituted as he hurt his foot.

PUPPY LOVE...

Darren Barnard could claim he was a victim of puppy love during his time at Barnsley – even though his dog made him barking mad. Barnard could have improved on his 201 appearances for the Tykes had he not been out of action for five months thanks to his canine friend. The player slipped in a puddle left by his puppy on the kitchen floor and suffered knee ligament damage.

WRIGHT WRONG

Richard Wright missed a couple of weeks' football after he fell out of the loft at his home.

Then the former Arsenal and Ipswich shot-stopper was ruled out of action with a twisted ankle he suffered in the warm up to a game – after he tripped over a sign in the goal-mouth warning players not to warm up in that area!

RING OF PAIN

Switzerland midfielder Paulo Diogo paid a heavy price for getting over-excited when his Servette side scored against Schaffhausen.

He jumped into metal fencing segregating the fans and his wedding ring got caught in the barrier.

His finger became detached and match officials were unable to find the digit. He was yellow carded for 'crowd-interference'!

FOWL PLAY

Former Juventus midfielder Ivano Bonetti ran foul of Grimsby boss Brian Laws. Laws was so annoyed at Bonetti's lack of performance in a defeat at Luton that he grabbed a plate of chicken wings – and hurled them into the Italian's face. The player suffered a fractured cheekbone and never appeared for the club again.

TYRED OUT

Midfielder Éver Banega decided that the best way to chill out before his Valencia side faced the might of Barcelona in a big cup game was to go for a short drive. He pulled into a petrol station to refuel but forgot to apply the car's handbrake and the vehicle rolled back trapping his leg. Banega was out of action for six months.

SHORT, SHARP PAINS….

- Defender Svein Grondalen withdrew from a Norway squad in 1977 when he collided with a sleeping moose during a jogging session. The moose charged at Grondalen putting him out of action with a leg injury.
- David Batty was a tough midfielder for England but suffered ankle ligament damage after being run over… by his three-year-old daughter riding her tricycle.
- Portsmouth hardman John Durnin was playing golf with teammate Alan McLoughlin when they failed to spot a fairway hollow and their buggy disappeared. Durnin suffered a dislocated elbow and was out of action for six weeks.
- Milan Rapaic once missed the opening to the Croatian League with Hajduk Split after he stuck a boarding pass into his eye at an airport!
- Keeper Chic Brodie's career was ended when he collided with a sheepdog that had run on to the pitch! The Brentford shot-stopper shattered a kneecap.

THE ONE-TEAM GAME

Scotland were involved in one of the craziest games ever played. In fact, it was a fixture they won – and drew!

The Tartan Army complained about the state of Estonia's floodlights when they were due to play an evening World Cup qualifier in 1996, so the kick-off was moved from 6.45 pm to 9 am.

Estonia were not happy and decided they wouldn't turn up for the fixture.

Scotland lined up against nobody, the national anthems were played and just three seconds after kick-off the game was called off and the visitors given a 3-0 victory by default.

FIFA, world football's governing body, later decided the game should be played out at a neutral venue and the two sides went through a no-score bore-draw in Monaco.

MISSING BEFORE ACTION

In 1950, before the use of substitutes was allowed, Yugoslavia started their game against Brazil with just ten men – after one of their players was injured before they even took to the pitch.

Rajko Mitic was so excited to be playing in the Maracana Stadium that he cracked his head on a girder in the changing room as he raced to the pitch.

Dazed, cut and bloodied, he missed the first 20 minutes of the game and wasn't even told until halftime that his side were already 1-0 down. They lost the match 2-0.

DARKEST AFRICA

Zaire (now DR Congo) became the first black African nation to qualify for the World

Cup when they competed in the 1974 finals in Germany. But they faced more than just opposition teams. The players were warned that if they lost by more than 4-0 against Brazil they would not be allowed to return home. The team had already been beaten 2-0 by Scotland and lost 9-0 against Yugoslavia.

Zaire leader Mobutu Sese Seko sent his presidential guards to see the team after the Yugoslavia result and issued the threat of not going home.

Zaire defender Mwepu Ilunga was so determined to ensure they didn't lose too heavily that he was booked after charging out of the defensive wall at a free kick to whack the ball upfield.

Although the players returned home without their wages and allowances they had been treated as heroes after qualifying. Mobutu had given all the players a car and a house and invited them to his own home for celebrations.

HEADS YOU LOSE

A goal down and with just 20 minutes to go Chile keeper Roberto Rojas thought he had a cunning plan to ensure his side might still qualify for the World Cup finals. Facing Brazil in the Maracana in 1989 the keeper retrieved a razor blade he had concealed in his gloves before the match and cut himself on the forehead before falling to the ground.

Blood streamed from the wound and a flare that had been thrown from the stands earlier in the game lay on the ground nearby. The shot-stopper's teammates carried him off the pitch and refused to play on claiming the conditions were not safe. But Rojas was caught out by television cameras that had recorded the flare landing a good distance from him – and he had also been captured cutting his own head.

Brazil were awarded a 2-0 win. Chile did not qualify for the 1990 tournament and were banned from the 1994 finals. Rojas was banned for life, although this was lifted in 2001 when he reached the age of 44.

CANINE CAPER

When England played Brazil in the 1962 World Cup play was interrupted when a small black dog got onto the pitch. Players and officials tried to catch the canine without luck before England forward Jimmy Greaves came up with a cunning plan. Greavsie got on all fours and managed to attract the mutt. But the dog was so scared that it peed over the player's shirt.

Brazil's Garrincha thought this was so funny that he took the dog home and kept it as a pet.

TRUE STORIES

- A match between Bena Tshadi and Basanaga in the DR Congo in 1998 ended with eleven players killed by a lightning strike. Thirty other people were seriously injured.
- Adrian Bastia of Asteras Tripolis grabbed a naked streaker during his side's clash with Panathinaikos but was then red-carded by the referee after the final whistle.
- The Manchester United side that lined up for an official team photo before their Champions League clash with Bayern Munich in 2001 contained an unusual face – labourer and Red Devils fan Karl Power, who had sneaked onto the pitch.

FANTASTIC FANS

Supporters are the lifeblood of any side. Meet some who have gone the extra mile… and more!

FAN POWER

A fan dying from cancer decided he'd suffered enough watching his favourite side struggle – and burst into their dressing room to tell them exactly what he thought of the players. Mark Saunders had seen Bristol City win just six games with around half the 2013-14 League One season gone.

So, with the blessing of boss Steve Cotterill he blasted out a few home truths to the players before their fixture with Gillingham. City won the game 2-1 and Mark reckoned it was the best match he had seen all season.

He told the team: "We, the fans, when we are out there, we have each other's backs, we help each other out. You guys need to work together as a team… You've got your wages and your fancy cars in the car park, just remember who you are playing for. This is our club. We follow you because we love the club. Get out there and win.'

ALL WHITE

Phil Beeton watched an amazing 2,000 Leeds United games in a row. From 1967 to 2014 he went to every home and away fixture, even European matches. Once he even flew back from a holiday in the Canary Islands so that he could see the Whites in action at Elland Road.

VINTAGE SUPPORT

Wine merchant Arrigo Brovedani was the ONLY Udinese fan to turn up for his side's game at Sampdoria in 2012. He was in town on business and initially got a hostile reception from the home support. But his team won 2-0 and after the game he was clapped and offered a meal by Sampdoria followers.

BOB'S JOB

Robert Nesbitt had an expensive and painful tattoo put on his thigh to celebrate the goal scoring feats of ace striker Andy Cole. But just two days later hitman Cole was sold by Newcastle United to Manchester United!

PLAYING UP FOR POMPEY

By day he's a respected bookshop owner. On match days he becomes Portsmouth's most noted fan. Having changed his name by deed poll in 1989 he is now known as John Portsmouth Football Club Westwood. You can't miss him at games as he rings a bell, is covered in Pompey tattoos and wears a stovepipe hat.

FOOT PROBLEM

Stuart Ansill watched 1,786 consecutive Nottingham Forest games over a period of 40 years – before doctors banned him from following his side to a match at Burnley. The pensioner reckoned he had travelled more than 100,000 miles by airplane, car and coach and had seen more than 2,500 matches involving his favourite side. Even when he was hospitalised with a foot infection he managed to get out in time to see his side play at the weekend. But medics told him he couldn't travel across country to see the next match at Burnley following an operation on the foot. For the first time in his life

Stuart had to listen to match commentary on a radio.

SUPER SUPPORTERS

- Paul Williams spent more than £8,000 to see Gosport FC play in the 2014 FA Trophy Final at Wembley. He flew from New Zealand to London only to see his favourite team lose 4-0 to Cambridge in the non-league cup final.

- A fan of Turkish side Galatasaray saved money by not buying his club's shirt and instead had the name of his favourite player – Didier Drogba – shaved into the hairs on his back!

- Rob Shannon saw more than 1,800 consecutive Birmingham City matches at home, Slovenia, Belgium and Portugal. But he missed a match against QPR in 1974 through illness.

- Convinced that Brazil superstar Kaka was set to sign for his favoured Manchester City side, fan Chris Atkinson had the forward's name tattooed on his chest. Kaka had a change of heart and stayed at AC Milan.

BALL BOYS WHO INFLUENCED GAMES

OH BOY!

Just like players, linesmen and referees, ball boys are part and parcel of football. Sometimes they get a bit more involved than they should…

GOAL BOY

It hasn't happened often but in 2006 a ball boy changed the result of a game.

Brazilian side Atlético Sorocaba were beating Santacruzense 1-0 with just minutes to go when a shot whizzed past their post.

Unseen by the female referee, Silvia Regina de Oliveira, a ball boy picked up the ball that had gone out of play and side-footed it into the goal.

When the ref turned around and saw where the ball was she gave a goal and the game finished 1-1.

The Brazilian FA allowed the result to stand but the official and linesmen were all suspended.

WHOSE BALL?

Ball boy Charlie Morgan became an Internet celebrity after being involved in a clash with Chelsea midfielder Eden Hazard.

Belgium international Hazard appeared to kick the boy during his side's League Cup semi-final game against Cardiff City in 2013.

Morgan had held onto the ball for longer than the Chelsea side would have liked and was thought to be time-wasting with Cardiff 2-0 up.

Hazard said: 'The boy put his whole body on to the ball and I was just trying to kick the ball. I think I kicked the ball and not the boy. I apologise.'

Hazard was banned for three games. Morgan, 17, was stopped from being a ball boy at a Wales international a few weeks later.

SPURRED ON

Tottenham fans, already happy with their side being 4-0 up, were cheering even more when a ball boy decided to help the home team further.

When the ball went out of play in Spurs' UEFA Cup game against Famagusta in 2007 the boy didn't just hand the ball back to the visitors he threw it with some venom… and directed at a player's private parts.

In another incident at White Hart Lane, a ball boy ran onto the pitch in a 2010 Premier League match against Bolton Wanderers and grabbed the ball even though it was still in play. The game was restarted with a dropped ball.

SHOUTING MATCH

Napoli keeper Morgan De Sanctis launched a verbal tirade at a ball boy whom he accused of throwing the ball into play too quickly. The Italian keeper, whose side beat Lecce 2-0, realised at halftime that he wasn't happy with the abuse he had handed out. He went and found the ball boy, kissed him and later gave the youngster his shirt.

TAKE THAT…

- Boca Unidos keeper Gaston Sessa was red-carded in Argentina after he kicked the ball into a ball boy's face at point blank range.
- Dario Fernandez of Panionios started a pitch brawl during a Greek game at PAOK when he pushed a home team ball boy. PAOK fans responded to the incident by throwing missiles at the midfielder. But the ball boy helped to remove the items, including bottles, from the pitch!
- During a match in Switzerland between Lausanne and FC Sion, away team striker Geoffroy Serey Die slapped a ball boy. The player was suspended for a record eight matches.
- Winger Colin Clark of LA Galaxy got a three-game suspension and a big fine for yelling anti-gay slurs at a ball boy in 2012.

TOP TRIVIA

SLEEPING GIANT

Spanish striker Michu revealed the secret of success – cider, beans and sleep. The hitman was a smash hit in the Premier League after his £2m move to Swansea City from Rayo Vallecano in 2012 and admits that whenever he can he likes a quick siesta. He also got his parents to boost his food supplies by travelling from Spain to Wales with fresh stocks of the ingredients for the bean stew that gives him firepower.

The 'fabada' (bean stew) contains beans, pork, chorizo sausage and saffron.

Michu also reckoned a few crates of locally brewed cider from his local Asturias area of northern Spain would also improve his game.

LUCKY WINNER

A 50 pence bet earned a massive £63,000 for a lucky football punter. But if the guy had increased his stake to £10 on the same games he would have collected a cool £1million! The man correctly predicted the outcome of 12 games in six different countries and his odds worked out at an amazing 126,322 to 1.

CLOTHES MAKETH MAN

Football coaches who wear suits on match days and tracksuits on training days are more likely to get the best out of their teams.

Dr Richard Thelwell of Portsmouth University said: "We have found that the clothing that coaches wear can have a direct effect on the players' perceptions of the coach's ability. Players look to their coach to provide technical skills, to motivate them and to lead them.

"A coach in a suit suggests strategic prowess—which is obviously ideal for a match. In our study, coaches wearing a suit were perceived as being more strategically competent than those wearing sporting attire. However, when wearing sporting attire, they were perceived to be more technically competent than those in a suit."

But a coach of large build and wearing smart clothes was ranked the lowest in terms of competence to motivate, develop technique, develop game strategy and build athlete character!

A coach who was lean and wearing a tracksuit was rated best for technical and character-building abilities!

LET'S CALL THEM THE CLUB...

How's this for what is believed to be the longest name in the world for a football team?

Translated properly Thai Pro League side would be called:

Krung Thep Mahanakhon Amon Rattanakosin Mahinthara Ayuthaya Mahadilok Phop Noppharat Ratchathani Burirom Udomratchaniwet Mahasathan Amon Piman Awatan Sathit Sakkathattiya Witsanukam Prasit Bravo Association Football Club!

Then there's always Bangkok University FC which would be: Samosorn Maha Vittiyalai Krungthep Mahanakorn Boworn Rattanakosin Mahintara Yutthaya Mahadilok Phop Noparat Rajathani Burirom Udom Rajaniwet Mahasatharn Amorn Phimarn Avatarn Sathit Sakkatattiya Vishnukarm Prasit.

Who would want to make a football commentary in Thai?

QUICK SHOTS

- Could Chelsea have some alien supporters from outer space? Secret government documents made public a few years ago reveal that a UFO was spotted over Stamford Bridge when the Blues played Manchester United in March 1999.

- Spain midfielder Juan Mata could have been a pop star if he hadn't turned his back on music to shine on a football pitch. Manchester United's record buy was such a good singer at school that his teacher tried to persuade him not to take up football!

- Mario Balotelli loves his friends and after he became joint top scorer at Euro 2012 he bought several of his mates super mini cars. The total bill was around £100,000.

- Paul Scholes left his car running – and it disappeared from outside his home! Manchester United's former England midfielder had been de-icing his windscreen when he popped indoors. When he came back the Chevrolet Captiva had been stolen from his drive.

- Legendary former Arsenal and England keeper David Seaman cut off his ridiculous ponytail back in 2005. But he's still got it… stuffed in a drawer at his home! He says that rather than auction if off for charity he has hung on to the hair just in case he wants to wear it again.

CHAPTER 9

GAME CHANGERS

WILD INCIDENTS FROM TOP FIXTURES

Amazing incidents that changed the outcome of football games. You couldn't make these up!

LIFE'S A BEACH

Liverpool's struggling start to season 2009-10 got even worse when they suffered an unexpected defeat at Sunderland – thanks to a beach ball!

Striker Darren Bent had a shot at goal after just five minutes and the match ball deflected off the beach ball and sent the keeper the wrong way to give the home side a 1-0 victory.

Ironically it was a Reds' fan who had thrown the ball onto the pitch at the Stadium of Light.

According to the rules of the game the referee should have disallowed the goal and awarded a dropped ball.

Sunderland boss Steve Bruce said: 'They have got it [the beach ball] on telly with the guy who threw it on and it's got Liverpool crests all over it. What a shame.'

Liverpool fan Callum Campbell, 16, later admitted: 'I'm the one who did it. I'm so, so sorry. This is my worst, worst nightmare. The beach ball wasn't even mine. The crowd were bouncing it around above their heads, then it came my way and I just took a big swing and knocked it towards the pitch. After that the wind carried it into the net.'

GAME IS SUNK!

Defender Kevan Brown was playing his usual reliable game as captain when his right leg disappeared! The Woking FC skipper was totally puzzled as to what had happened then realised that a giant hole had appeared in his team's Kingfield pitch.

Forget the jokes about someone playing in the hole - this one became deep enough to swallow a player!

Officials halted the Conference game against Hayes in season 1996-97 after just 20 minutes as they pondered on a solution. Someone had the brainwave of pouring a bucket of sand down the hole. That all disappeared!

More earth and sand were put into the gaping crevice but still it did not fill up and the game had to be abandoned. Investigations revealed an ancient drainage system beneath the turf had collapsed and more holes were about to appear.

BALLOON GOES UP

Jamaica striker Luton Shelton not only beat the opposition in an FA Cup tie – he also had to outfox a number of balloons.

Loads of balloons that had been thrown on at the start of the game were still hanging around the pitch and a number of them were in the Manchester City penalty area.

Shelton beat the balloons to score after the ball had bounced off one of them and confused City's Michael Ball.

Shelton's goal helped Sheffield United to a surprise 2-1 win over City in the third round tie in January 2008.

"I suppose it makes for a good story—a Jamaican coming over here from Sweden and picking his way through the balloons to score a goal against one of England's top teams in the FA Cup," said Shelton.

LOST IN THE FOG...

To get football up and running again at the end of World War II the Football Association decided to invite Dynamo Moscow to England for a tour in 1945.

But the outcome of the club's final friendly, against Arsenal, could easily have sparked more troubles!

Dynamo brought their own referee but his problems were heightened by a thick fog that shrouded White Hart Lane, Tottenham's ground being used for the match as Arsenal's Highbury was still under military control. After just 30 seconds the Russians took the lead, though few of the 55,000 crowd saw the goal because of the fog.

Although the game ended 3-3 there was also mass confusion because of the weather conditions.

The Russians are believed to have had 12 players or more on the pitch after failing to take off players when substitutions were made.

Arsenal also reportedly had a sent-off player on the pitch when he used the lack of visibility to sneak back into action.

And the Gunners' keeper knocked himself out when he ran into the mist-shrouded goal post – although a spectator is said to have jumped from the stands and taken his place!

SOME YOU CAN'T WIN

Chris Nicholl scored all four of the goals in an Aston Villa v Leicester City fixture – yet still wasn't on the winning side!

The Villa defender scored two for his club and two own-goals for the Foxes in March 1976 as the game ended 2-2.

'The third goal, Leicester's second, was a cracker", he said. 'Best goal I ever scored. A diving header. No goalkeeper would have saved that.'

Nicholl asked the referee at the end of the game if he could keep the match ball, but the official refused as it was the last game of his own career and he wanted it as a memento!

BEAT THAT!

How do you win 149-0 without even scoring a goal? Here's the answer...

In the Madagascar League, Stade Olympique de L'Emyrne were held 2-2 by DSA in one of the final games of the season, a controversial late penalty costing them victory.

The result meant Stade could not beat AS Adema – who they played next – to the title. In protest, Stade kept on scoring own goals when they faced their championship rivals. But their football association were not impressed by the 149-0 result.

The FA suspended Stade's coach, Zake Be, for three years and all of the players from both teams got an official warning.

Still, they got into the record books for the biggest defeat in professional football!

THE KEEPER'S SCORED

He's meant to keep out the shots but sometimes the goalkeeper decides he'd like to be on the scoresheet. Here are just a few of the scoring shot-stoppers!

TON-UP CENI

Brazilian keeper Rogério Ceni would put a lot of top-class strikers to shame when it comes to netting goals.

The Sao Paolo shot-stopper has netted more than 100 goals – the first keeper to do so – and at the age of 41 was still turning out for his one and only club in 2013–14.

Admittedly he's got the goals from penalties and free kicks but putting the ball in the back of the net is what wins matches!

Ceni began his professional career in 1992 and won 16 caps for Brazil. Although he didn't score for his country he did turn out in two World Cups. He's played a record number of games for Sao Paolo – more than 1,100 – and scored in every major tournament in which the club has played.

Among his honours are three Brazilian league titles, a Club World Cup, Intercontinental Cup, two Brazilian Footballer of the Year Awards and best keeper in Brazil's Serie A on six occasions.

He was also part of Brazil's World Cup 2002 winning squad, although he did not appear in the final against Germany.

BULLDOG BITES!

If you had a player on your books who had scored 67 league and cup goals – including eight at international level – there's a fair bet he was an attacking midfielder or a not-too-prolific striker.

But José Luis Chilavert got all of his strikes playing as a keeper.

During a professional career that ran from 1982 to 2004 he scored while playing in Paraguay, Uruguay, Argentina and Spain but failed during his time in France.

Most of his goals at club level came during his time with Argentine side Vélez Sarsfield, and included 36 league strikes.

The man nicknamed 'The Bulldog' because of his temper—received a suspended three-month prison sentence and an 18-month ban from soccer for punching a stadium official in Argentina—also struck eight goals in 74 games for Paraguay.

After he hung up his gloves the controversial stopper, the first keeper to score a hat trick in a game, claimed: 'I don't know what a Chilavert would be worth at today's prices, but I'm sure it'd be a lot of money. There aren't many keepers who can go forward and score goals.'

SMASHING GLASS

Jimmy Glass wrote his name in football folklore with a history-making goal.

On loan from Swindon Town to Carlisle United, Glass was between the sticks for a crunch home game against Plymouth Argyle. Carlisle had to win the fixture to stay in the Football League. If they didn't they would be relegated to the Conference.

With the game five minutes into injury time the two sides were locked at 1-1 as the Cumbrians looked set for non-league the following season.

Then Carlisle were awarded a corner. All 22 players on the pitch were in the Argyle penalty box – including Glass, who had left his goal at the other end. The ball came over, bobbled about and then was struck right-footed by Glass into the bottom corner. The goal came with the last kick of the game and ensured Carlisle retained League status.

THE MADMAN!

With his wild curly hair René Higuita looked eccentric – and was nicknamed 'El Loco', The Madman, by his teammates.

The Colombia keeper was famed for his 'Scorpion Kick', a save that involved him falling forward, curling back his feet and kicking the ball back over his head using his heels.

Rather than just catch a ball or lump it away he often left his teammates wondering what was going to happen next when he tried to play as a defender and dribble the ball out of the box.

After a career that stretched from 1985–2010 he finished with 41 club goals and another seven at international level from his 68 appearances for Colombia.

SCORE AND SAVE

Former England keeper Paul Robinson scored goals for two different clubs – including one in the Premier League. Robinson was playing a League Cup tie for Leeds United when he headed the equaliser against Swindon late in the game to take the match to extra time.

He then saved a penalty in a shootout to ensure Leeds won the game in 2003–04. Robinson was Player of the Year that season, nominated by the Leeds' fans.

In March 2007, playing for Tottenham against Watford in the Premier League, Robbo launched a free kick almost level with his own penalty area which went over the head of opposition keeper Ben Foster, his international rival at the time.

'I've experienced this sort of thing and it's not nice', said Robinson. 'I'll try not to mention it in [England] training next week – ha, ha!'

SPOT ON...

- Bulgarian keeper Dimitar Ivanko hit 42 penalties during his career from 1996–2011, playing for Levski Sofia, Kayserispor and Bursaspor.
- German keeper Hans-Jorg Butt scored 32 goals between 1994 and 2012, which included three goals in the Champions League, a record.
- Ian Turner kept three clean sheets in a row for Preston North End – and also got himself on the score sheet with a goal from his own penalty area. He drop-kicked a ball and it went over the head of his opposite number in the Notts County goal!

MIGHTY MISTAKES:
MATCHES THAT ENDED WITH THE WRONG SCORE

Technology is now settling some disputes about whether the ball has crossed the line or not. But some major games could have ended with far different outcomes if goal-line technology had been in use…

ARGENTINA V ENGLAND, WORLD CUP, 1986

The Hand of God goal! Diego Maradona sensationally used his palm to score for Argentina.

Maradona challenged England keeper Peter Shilton for the ball and clearly punched it into the back of the net.

Referee Ali Bin Nasser signalled a goal, Argentina were 1-0 up and went on to win 2-0 thanks to a brilliant solo effort, also from Maradona.

Peter Reid, England midfielder, said: 'We could all see it was handball. Terry Fenwick, Terry Butcher, Glenn Hoddle and me, we were swearing at the Tunisian ref but we were talking to a brick wall. ...In my mind, Shilts [Shilton] should have just taken his head off. Then Maradona wouldn't have scored and would have had too big a headache to have dribbled round five of us for the second three minutes later.'

LIVERPOOL V CHELSEA, CHAMPIONS LEAGUE SEMI-FINAL, 2005

The Premier League sides didn't produce the great game expected but the fixture will be remembered for Luis Garcia's controversial winning goal.

The referee reckoned the Spaniard's shot had crossed the line despite television replays revealing William Gallas had stopped it going over.

Liverpool won this second leg 1-0 and went through to the final.

Chelsea manager Jose Mourinho said: 'The best team lost. That's for sure. They score – if you can say that—they score. We can say the linesman scored. So they were in a position of 1-0 up, and they just defend. They did it well. They were lucky.'

MANCHESTER UNITED V TOTTENHAM, PREMIER LEAGUE, 2005

With just two minutes remaining and no score Spurs almost recorded a famous win at Old Trafford. Portugal midfielder Pedro Mendes struck the ball from the halfway line and caught keeper Roy Carroll off his line. The ball crossed the line but Carroll clawed it out and play continued.

Linesman Rob Lewis said: 'The Spurs player shot from distance and I was doing my primary job, which was to stand in line with the last defender and watch for an offside. …There was nothing I could have done differently apart from run faster than Linford Christie. …When the ball landed I was still 25 yards from goal and it was impossible to judge if it had crossed the line.'

WATFORD V READING, CHAMPIONSHIP, 2008

Referee Stuart Attwell gave the opening goal to Reading 13 minutes into this game on the advice of Nigel Bannister, one of his assistants.

TV replays showed the ball had crossed the line four or five feet wide of a post following a corner. The match ended 2-2.

Reading forward Stephen Hunt admitted: 'If it happened to us, we'd have been fuming, but you have to try to control yourselves, even if you are disappointed and gutted… I was trying to claim the goal after he gave it. You can't say, "Hold on ref, don't give us a goal".'

IRELAND V FRANCE, WORLD CUP PLAY-OFF, 2009

Ireland had controlled the game and took the lead through Robbie Keane, which meant the game was tied on aggregate as France had won the first leg.

France attacked and striker Thierry Henry pushed the ball back into play with his hand after it had crossed the byline – then William Gallas headed home to win the match for France. Henry later admitted the handball.

Ireland manager Giovanni Trapattoni said: 'All European people saw the situation. I am sure that, if the referee had asked Henry, he would have admitted to the handball. …I would prefer to go out on penalties than this. I am sad because the referee had the time to ask the linesman and Henry.'

BRISTOL CITY V CRYSTAL PALACE, CHAMPIONSHIP, 2009

Striker Freddie Sears, on loan from West Ham, hammered the ball into the back of the net for Crystal Palace.

But he slammed the ball so hard it came back out of the goal and referee Rob Shoebridge waved play on believing the ball had not crossed the line.

City won 1-0 with a 90th-minute strike.

Neil Warnock, Palace manager, said: 'We were cheated. And I'm not saying that against the referee because he didn't mean to get it wrong. …We can put a man on the moon, time serves of 100 miles per hour at Wimbledon, yet we cannot place a couple of sensors in a net to show when a goal has been scored. …I feel sorry for the referee because he didn't get any help. But how can I mark him when he spoils an otherwise good display with a mistake of that importance?'

ENGLAND V GERMANY, WORLD CUP, 2010

England were losing 2-1 when midfielder Frank Lampard chipped German keeper Manuel Neuer. The ball clipped the bar and bounced over the line. Uruguayan referee Jorge Larrionda disagreed and waved play on.

England would have gone in to the half-time break at 2-2. Instead they came out for the second half downhearted and lost 4-1.

Lampard said: 'I still get asked about it. It wasn't Germany's fault, that's for sure. It was a mistake by the referee and it has created a change because now we have goal-line technology, which is one bonus. It happened, it's history.'

MANCHESTER UNITED V TOTTENHAM, PREMIER LEAGUE, 2010

With six minutes to go, Tottenham were 1-0 down and looking for an equaliser. Their keeper Heurelho Gomes threw the ball to the floor for a clear free kick believing Nani had handled.

But the referee did not blow for an infringement and United winger Nani took the ball and knocked it into the net. Tottenham boss Harry Redknapp said: 'The whole thing was a farce. It was handball. Nani put his hand on it and dragged it down. Mark Clattenburg is a top referee but he had a nightmare with that.'

MENTAL MASCOTS: FURRY, FUNNY AND CRACKERS

They're soft, furry, loveable...and sometimes bonkers and dangerous.

SWAN SONG

Cyril the Swan is a top bird, having flown up from the lower divisions into the Premier League with Swansea City. But he's also made his mark during fights with other mascots and stewards and even appeared in court for his bad behaviour. Cyril has starred in pantomime, has his own replica soft toys on sale in the club shop, been fined and even been in bother for leading a pitch invasion. One of his worst attacks came when he ripped the head off Millwall mascot Zampa the Lion and kicked it along the ground.

MONKEY BUSINESS

H'Angus Monkey, mascot to Hartlepool United. The mascot's monkey outfit refers to an animal that was found on the local beach during the First World War and then hanged as a spy.

The monkey suit was once worn by Stuart Drummond, later to become the town's mayor, whose campaign included an offer of free bananas to school children.

H'Angus's monkey business once got him ejected from the Victoria Ground for leading fans in a singsong.

DRAGON SNUFFED

Rochdale's Desmond Dragon wasn't happy when he saw Freddie Fox of Halifax cock his leg up against his side's goal post.

Freddie had pulled Desmond's tail earlier and been pushed backward into the goal before cocking his leg. The Dragon's threat was snuffed out by police who ejected him from the ground.

NAKED TRUTH

Bertie Bee may be soft, furry and appealing but he can carry quite a sting!

When a streaker ran across the pitch during Burnley's match against Preston, Bertie buzzed into action. As the naked man avoided capture by stewards, Bertie ran into his path, upped him over his shoulder and put the intruder flat on the ground. The Burnley mascot then did a butterfly swimming stroke along the touchline to celebrate nabbing the streaker.

LION HEART

Reading's Kingsley Lion was sent off by referee Mike Riley!

The man in black reckoned that the mascot in the blue and white-hooped shirt was confusing him because he looked too much like a Reading player! Come on! He's eight foot tall and in a lion's outfit! Yet manager Steve Coppell said: 'He does look like so many of my players.'

Kingsley was also sent-of for a handball and was once flattened by Royals' captain Graeme Murty, a fight that left the mascot without a head!

OWL ABOUT THAT?

Chaddy the Owl was ejected during his Oldham side's game at Doncaster for allegedly trying to start a riot. But he had previous form for scrapping with Blackpool's Bloomfield Bear during a halftime battle. Chaddy threw the bear's giant boots into the crowd, which led to a six-month investigation by police who then decided to take no further action.

MORE MAD LADS...

- Before Darlington crashed out of league existence their Darlo Dog was in the doghouse for playing up in front of the TV cameras, body surfing on advertising hoardings and rolling around during a game. He was escorted from the ground but was allowed back in for the club's next fixture.
- Robbie the Bobby, Bury FC's rogue policeman, copped sendings off for twice showing his backside to rival fans, fighting with Cardiff's Bluebird and yanking at the ears of the Peterborough rabbit, Peter Burrow!
- Paisley the Panda from St. Mirren was so bad that he got the sack! Among his stunts were pretending to use a rival team's shirt as toilet paper, whacking supporters with an inflatable sheep, disrupting a pre-match warm up and insulting visiting fans and players.
- Port Vale mascot Boomer the Dog gave away the bride when Nicola Williamson married club fan Dave Walker. The groom didn't even know it was going to happen!

- Aston Villa sacked Hercules the Lion for "inappropriate and unprofessional behaviour" during a Premier League game against Crystal Palace. The mascot had hugged and kissed Miss Aston Villa, Debbie Robins.
- Fulham's Billy Badger was escorted from the pitch by referee Chris Hoy after break dancing and causing a delay to the second half of a game.

KIT CLANGERS: WHEN THE SHIRTS DIDN'T FIT

Teams usually have a home and away kit and often a third shirt for cup games. Pretty easy to decide what to wear against the opposition then… well, that's not always been the case!

A GREY DAY

One of the most infamous Premier League shirts of all-time was the grey away shirt Manchester United launched for 1995-96 season. It was so bad that manager Sir Alex Ferguson blamed it for a dramatic slump in results. His side lost four games and drew another while wearing the shirt that was dubbed 'the invisible kit'. Things got so bad that when the Reds were trailing 3-0 at halftime at Southampton Fergie made his side change their kit.

Sir Alex, whose side still lost 3-1, claimed: "The players couldn't pick each other out. They said it was difficult to see their teammates at distance when they lifted their heads."

A poll of fans for the *Manchester Evening News* resulted in the grey shirt being branded United's worst kit of all time.

ANYONE REMEMBER THE BALL?

When you play golf you take clubs; when you go fishing and you take rods – but when Millwall travelled to Sheffield Wednesday in 2013-14 their kit man forgot their shirts!

Boss Steve Lomas sent a message back to the Lions' ground in South London asking for kit to be rushed up the motorway to Yorkshire.

But the shirts failed to arrive at Wednesday's Hillsborough ground in time for kick-off and Millwall, who normally pull on blue, had to wear the home side's yellow away kit from the previous campaign.

Wednesday were victims to the change shirt syndrome when they visited Tranmere Rovers in 2000-01.

Both their blue home kit and white away kit were deemed unsuitable against Tranmere's usual blue and white.

So the Owls had to wear Rovers' dark blue away shirt and were beaten 2-0.

BLUES ALL ROUND

It was a case of signing the blues when Chelsea arrived at Coventry City for a game in 1996-97.

The visitors had only taken their usual blue home kit and the referee delayed the kick-off because City were in the light blue shirts that gives them their Sky Blues nickname.

Following a 15-minute debate Chelsea pulled on the not very highly-rated red and black Coventry kit. To make matters worse the team nicknamed the Blues were beaten 3-1.

BARGAIN HUNT

You couldn't make it up… a game was put on hold while a club official went to buy shirts from a market stall.

Independiente Santa Fe had arrived at Boyaca Chico in the Colombian Primer A League without their away kit and discovered their regular shirts clashed with the home side.

The home team refused to wear their own away kit so Santa Fe sent one of their officials shopping.

As puzzled fans wondered what was happening, the official found a market stall that was selling counterfeit football shirts at knockdown prices and bought a full team kit.

He then hotfooted it back to the ground where players used a marker pen to write their names and numbers on the backs of the shirts.

The referee gave the game the go-ahead and Santa Fe won 2-0.

DON A NEW SHIRT

Oxford United have form when it comes to changing their kit on the road.

In season 1998-99 they went to Watford with their usual yellow home shirts, which clashed with the Hornets kit, and had to borrow the home side's blue away gear.

In 2005-06 they did have their black away kit with them when they visited Barnet… but the home side had changed to a black home shirt for that season. Oxford played the game in Barnet's old orange shirt.

That same season they went to Boston United and before they travelled they got the thumbs-up from the referee that they could wear their usual yellow.

Fans were puzzled when their team appeared in Boston youth side's blue and white shirt. The man in black had changed his mind and claimed Oxford's yellow would clash with Boston's home kit.

A RIGHT CHARLIE...

Bayern Munich kitman Charlie Ehmann was certain his club's Champions League opponents Cologne would be wearing white.

It seemed a safe bet as the last ten times Bayern had been to Cologne the home side had been in that colour.

But just an hour before kick-off Bayern discovered their opponents would be in red shirts and socks with white shorts.

The visitors had traveled with their wine red shirts, dark grey shorts and both those colours in the socks… and the referee reckoned there would be too much of a colour clash between the teams.

Kick-off was delayed and with no spare kit in sight things looked bleak until Bayern staff discovered white practise bibs in their kit. Even better, these were adorned with the logo of their sponsors Opel.

Cologne, who had refused to change to white, were beaten 2-0 and at the end of the season were relegated.

QUICK CHANGES

- France faced Hungary at the 1978 World Cup wearing the green and white hooped shirt of local Argentine side Kimberley, because television was worried about colour clashes.
- Both sides in the 1952 Irish Cup Final had to borrow kit from other teams

when they turned up in hooped tops, both containing red. Ards wore a Linfield strip and Glentoran pulled on a Cliftonville top.

- Carlisle United had to wear Rochdale's away kit in two successive years when they visited Spotland.

- Sheffield United were forced to wear Colchester's away kit in 1982 because their own shirts carried the logo of sponsors, which, at that time, was not permitted on television.

ANIMAL ANTICS

You've heard the expressions that footballers can be barking mad or lay on the purrfect pass. But sometimes it's real animals that have had a big influence of major football matches…

The Anfield Cat

Liverpool's Premier League stars were overshadowed in February 2012 by the arrival of a football feline at their Anfield ground. The grey and white tabby pounded up and down the touchline in warm-up fashion before strolling onto the pitch during the game against Tottenham.

Previously spotted on a number of occasions prowling around outside the ground the stray moggie even held up play as it ventured toward Spurs keeper Brad Friedel.

The cat, which was caught by a steward and released outside of the stadium, was nicknamed Kenny, after manager and Liverpool legend Kenny Dalglish. Some 44,000 fans in the ground chanted 'Cat' and then more than 50,000 people followed a spoof Twitter account dedicated to the moggy.

KICK WAS NO HOOT

Panama defender Luis Moreno received death threats after he attacked an owl that invaded a football match. The bird landed on the pitch during a game in Colombia between Deportivo Pereira and Junior Barranquilla and was then hit by the ball.

Deportivo's Moreno claimed he then kicked the bird, which later died, in a bid to check if it was still alive. The owl had been the unofficial mascot of Barranquilla.

Moreno was banned for two games, fined, had to pay veterinary costs and ordered to do community service at a local zoo.

FELLED BY A PINE

Keeper David Da Costa was called in to save the day when a vicious pine marten invaded a game in Switzerland. The match between FC Thun and Zurich was held up when the creature ran around the pitch for about five minutes – and then bit Zurich defender Loris Benito, drawing blood, as he tried to capture it.

Da Costa, his hands covered in his keeper's gloves, was able to grab the pine marten.

DOG DAYS

Football in Argentina has been dogged by bad luck.

José Jiménez of Bella Vista was pelted by objects thrown from the crowd after he grabbed a stray pooch by the neck and then heaved it off the pitch.

Opposition players from San Juan confronted Jiménez, who was red-carded, after he threw the dog into a fence before it was able to run away.

A game between Rosario Central and River Plate in Argentina's top-flight was halted in 2014 when a dog ran onto the pitch and used the grass as a toilet.

Play was held up for five minutes as an official carried the dog off – and another had to scoop the poop!

OUT-FOXED

Players in Glasgow's Old Firm derby were outshone by a crafty fox! The bushy tailed beast evaded capture by Rangers and Celtic players as it ran around the pitch at Celtic Park in 1996. In fact, it was so fast that it made its own getaway and was never seen again.

PITCH INVADERS…

- Zulte-Waregem's Mouhamadou Habib Habibou had to remove a duck from the pitch during a Belgian League game in 2010.
- A chicken led players a merry dance as they tried to catch it during the European Cup Winners' Cup clash between Dynamo Kiev and Atlético Madrid in 1986.
- A squirrel visited the Emirates Stadium pitch during Arsenal's home Champions League tie against Villarreal in 2006.

TOP TRIVIA

COLD COMFORT

First footballers wore long sleeved shirts, followed by gloves and even scarves! But the player who really stood out was Blackburn defender Pascal Chimbonda who admitted: 'In training, when it's very cold, I wear one pair or gloves, but during games I will wear two. I started to wear them because when I joined it was a very cold winter.'

Mind you, West Ham striker Alessandro Diamanti was spotted wearing a neck warmer during a game.

WEB WATCH

Hard-man defenders didn't worry England striker Darren Bent. And rough and tumble strikers didn't make Sheffield Wednesday's Frank Simek flinch. But both of them have a dreaded fear of... spiders!

'Don't get me started on spiders; they terrify me', added the 1.8m (5ft 11in) tall Bent.

And former Arsenal youngster Simek, a USA international, confessed: "Spiders! My grandpa got bitten by one and it was poisonous. To say what such a little thing can do to a person is frightening."

Maybe neither would fancy playing against Newcastle and Argentina winger Jonas Gutierrez – when he scores he has been known to pull on a Spiderman mask!

And they had both better not watch the film *Arachnophobia* – as a footballer dies in that movie after being bitten by a spider!

SPAIN PAIN

Shaun McCormack was gutted when Fernando Torres was transferred from Liverpool to Chelsea for a British record £50m.

The Reds' fan had just changed his name to Fernando Torres in praise of his hero! Days before the Spain striker made his move to Stamford Bridge, Shaun got the documentation through for his name change.

Shaun, 36, from Scunthorpe, had originally planned to rename himself Steven Gerrard, the Anfield captain, but he thought that would have been a bit plain and wanted something "a little more flamboyant".

Meanwhile, a Bulgarian fan had a 15-year legal battle before he was able to change his name to Mr Manchester Zdravkov Levidzhov-United.

SPOOKY BUT TRUE!

How's this for coincidences about two former England captains?

- John Terry was born on the same East London estate as Bobby Moore.
- As youngsters, both played for the same district side in Essex.
- The two captains played at the centre of defence and skippered both club and country.
- Bobby Moore died of cancer in 1993 but JT has given his backing to the Fund set up by Moore's widow Stephanie to fight the disease.
- The two stars both had 6 on the back of their shirts – although admittedly JT has 26!

CHAPTER 10

MEMORABLE MOMENTS, BIGGEST WINS AND IMPORTANT LISTS

TEN MEMORABLE MOMENTS

1. GAZZA'S TEARS AT ITALIA '90

Paul 'Gazza' Gascoigne was without doubt a genius footballer. But he was also, in the words of his England manager Sir Bobby Robson 'daft as a brush'.

But it was the tears he shed when he was booked in the 1990 World Cup semi-final that are unforgettable. Gazza realised that if England had beaten Germany the yellow card he received meant he would miss the final. He needn't have cried… England lost the semi on penalties.

2. SMILES BETTER

Six years later Gazza brought smiles all round to England fans when he used his left foot to flick the ball over the head of Scotland defender Colin Hendry at Euro '96. The Wembley crowd then watched in amazement as Gascoigne waltzed around the Scotland player and scored with a right foot volley.

3. SIX OF THE BEST

Scoring a hat trick is memorable. Getting two hat tricks in one game in amazing. But George Best lived up to his surname when he hit six goals for Manchester United against Northampton in February 1970. It was an FA Cup fourth round tie that United won 8-2 and Best scored with headers, flicks and dribbles to set a then scoring best for the competition.

4. WAR GAMES

The Falklands War had made Argentina v England a football battle between old enemies so when the sides met in the last 16 of World Cup 1998 there was an edge to the game. Argentina went ahead in the fourth minute through a Batistuta penalty before Michael Owen, making only his fourth start for England, won a spot-kick from which Alan Shearer equalised after 16 minutes. Then the 18-year-old hit the winner, a goal rightly acclaimed as one of England's best-ever and a strike Owen rates as one of his own best. Liverpool striker Owen was fed the ball by Beckham, ran past two experienced defenders and then smashed his strike past the keeper.

5. REPUBLIC RULE

The Republic of Ireland qualified for their first World Cup finals in 1990 – and made the planet sit up and take notice of their abilities. Managed by Jack Charlton, a World Cup winner with England, the Irish drew their three group games, against England, Egypt and Holland, and then won a penalty shootout against Romania to reach the quarter-finals.

They then faced hosts Italy and lost 1-0. The Irish had failed to win, had scored just two goals but were just one game away from the semi-finals at their first finals!

6. THE CLASS OF '96

England 4 Holland 1. That result of this group game at Wembley in the finals of Euro 96 says it all. England only needed a draw to reach the last eight but turned on the style with two goals each from Alan Shearer (one penalty) and Teddy Sheringham.

7. ROKER CHOKER

Sunderland were the small fry side from Roker Park who had no chance of beating the mighty Leeds United in the 1973 FA Cup Final. Except they did! The game was as memorable for the double-save by Sunderland keeper Jim Montgomery as it was for the goal by Ian Porterfield and the final result of 1-0.

8. SECONDS OUT...

It was the game that would decide where the English league title would go in 1989. Liverpool and Arsenal were the top two teams in the division and met in the final game of the season at Anfield. The Gunners needed to win by at least two goals – and Liverpool had not lost at home by two or more goals for three years. And it was 15 years since Arsenal had won at Anfield.

Alan Smith put the visitors ahead on 52 minutes.

Iin injury time at the end of the game Michael Thomas picked up the ball in midfield, ran into the penalty area and put the ball past on-coming keeper Grobbelaar. Two-nil to the Gunners with just 25 seconds left to play.

Arsenal and Liverpool finished level on points and goal difference. Arsenal lifted the title having scored eight goals more than the Reds.

9. GOAL RUSH

To score four goals in a professional game is amazing. To hit four in a massive derby-day fixture such as Everton v Liverpool is the stuff of dreams.

Ian Rush achieved that remarkable tally for the Reds against the Toffees in November 1982. He scored one in the first half and a hat trick in the second as Liverpool won 5-0 at Goodison Park, the home of Everton!

10. ALL THINGS MUST END...

Arsenal went a full season of 38 games unbeaten and lifted the 2003-04 Premier League title. Their amazing run of not losing stretched for a record 49 games between May 2002 and October 2004. During that time they won 36 and drew 13.

The fantastic run of the side that became known as 'The Invincibles' ended in a 2-0 defeat at Manchester United in October 2004.

ALL FIGURES CORRECT TO END OF SEASON 2013-14.

LISTS

PREMIER LEAGUE'S BIGGEST WINS	
Manchester United 9 Ipswich Town 0	March 1995
Tottenham Hotspur 9 Wigan Athletic 1	November 2009
Chelsea 8 Wigan Athletic 0	May 10
Chelsea 8 Aston Villa 0	December 2012
Newcastle United 8 Sheffield Wednesday 0	September 1999
Middlesbrough 8 Manchester City 1	May 2008
Nottingham Forest 1 Manchester United 8	February 1999
Chelsea 7 Stoke City 0	April 2010
Arsenal 7 Everton 0	May 2005
Blackburn Rovers 7 Nottingham Forest 0	November 1995
Manchester United 7 Barnsley 0	October 1997
Arsenal 7 Middlesbrough 0	January 2006
Manchester City 7 Norwich City 0	November 2013

FOOTBALL LEAGUE'S BIGGEST WINS		
Aston Villa 12 Accrington Stanley 2	March 1892	Division One
Manchester City 11 Lincoln City 3	March 1895	Division Two
Stockport County 13 Halifax 0	January 1934	Division Three (North)
Tranmere Rovers 13 Oldham 4	December 1935	Division Three (North)
Newcastle United 13 Newport County 0	October 1946	Division Two
Tottenham Hotspur 10 Everton 4	October 1958	Division One

MOST GOALS IN A LEAGUE GAME	
10 Joe Payne, Luton Town v Bristol Rover	April 1936
9 Bunny Bell, Tranmere Rovers v Oldham Athletic	December 1935
7 Ted Drake, Arsenal v Aston Villa	December 1935
7 Tim Coleman, Stoke City v Lincoln City	February 1957
7 Tommy Briggs, Blackburn v Bristol Rovers	February 1955

PREMIER LEAGUE GOLDEN BOOT WINNERS	
1993 Teddy Sheringham	Tottenham 22
1994 Andy Cole	Manchester United 34
1995 Alan Shearer	Blackburn Rovers 34
1996 Alan Shearer	Blackburn Rovers 31
1997 Alan Shearer	Newcastle United 25
1998 Chris Sutton	Blackburn Rovers; Dion Dublin, Coventry City; Michael Owen, Liverpool; all 18
1999 Michael Owen	Liverpool; Dwight Yorke, Manchester United; Jimmy Floyd-Hasselbaink, Leeds United; all 18
2000 Kevin Phillips	Sunderland 30
2001 Jimmy Floyd-Hasselbaink	Chelsea 23
2002 Thierry Henry	Arsenal 24
2003 Ruud van Nistelrooy	Manchester United 25
2004 Thierry Henry	Arsenal 30
2005 Thierry Henry	Arsenal 25
2006 Thierry Henry	Arsenal 27
2007 Didier Drogba	Chelsea 20
2008 Cristiano Ronaldo	Manchester United 31
2009 Nicolas Anelka	Chelsea 19
2010 Didier Drogba	Chelsea 29
2011 Carlos Tevez	Manchester City 20
2012 Robin van Persie	Arsenal 30
2013 Robin van Persie	Manchester United 26
2014 Luis Suárez	Liverpool 31

FOOTBALL LEAGUE'S BIGGEST AWAY WINS		
Port Vale 0 Sheffield United 10	December 1892	Division Two
Wolverhampton Wanderers 0 West Bromwich Albion 8	December, 1893	Division One
Newcastle 1 Sunderland 9	December 1908	Division One
Bristol City 0 Derby County 8	September 1923	Division Two
Accrington Stanley 0 Barnsley 9	February 1934	Division Three (North)
Northampton Town 0 Walsall 8	April 1947	Division Three (South)
Cardiff City 1 Wolverhampton Wanderers 9	September 1955	Division One
Halifax Town 0 Fulham 8	September 1969	Division Three
Barnet 1 Peterborough 9	September 1998	Division Three

MOST CLEAN SHEETS IN A SEASON		
(46 games unless stated)		
30 Port Vale	1953-54	Division Three (North)
29 Gillingham	1995-96	Division Three
28 Liverpool	1978-79	Division One (42 games)
27 Middlesbrough	1986-87	Division Three
27 Plymouth Argyle	2001-02	Division Three
26 Swindon Town	2011-12	League Two
26 Notts County	2009-10	League Two
26 Sunderland	1995-96	Division One
26 Aston Villa	1971-72	Division Three
26 Reading	1978-79	Division Four
26 Southampton	1921-22	Division Three (South) (42 games)
26 Rochdale	1923-24	Division Three (North) (42 games)

World's Top Ten Dirtiest Footballers and Their Playing Years	
1. Kevin Muscat	Australia (1989-2012)
2. Pepe	Portugal (2001-)
3. David Navarro	Spain (1999-)
4. Andoni Goikoetxea	Spain (1974-90)
5. Luis Suárez	Uruguay (2005-)
6. Gennaro Gattuso	Italy (1995-2013)
7. Roy Keane	Republic of Ireland (1989-2006)
8. Mark van Bommel	Holland (1992-2013)
9. Marco Materazzi	Italy (1993-2011)
10. Nigel de Jong	Holland (2002-)
* El Gol Digital	December 2013

BIG TWITTS	
Social media site Twitter is a direct line between many top players and fans. Here are some of the stars with the biggest followings.	
Robin van Persie	Manchester United: Followers: 4.9m
Joey Barton	QPR: Followers: 2.5m
Rio Ferdinand	Manchester United: Followers: 5.4m
Wayne Rooney	Manchester United: Followers: 8.5m
Cesc Fabregas	Barcelona: Followers: 6.5m
Cristiano Ronaldo	Real Madrid: Followers: 25.7m
Neymar	Barcelona: Followers: 10.5m

*All details correct May, 2014.

ABOUT THE AUTHOR:

Colin Mitchell admits he was always the fat kid at school who got shoved into goal and dreamed of the day he would get the chance to play as a striker. He did eventually squeeze his way out from between the sticks to play as a defender – but his biggest break came at the age of 16 when he broadcast live football reports on BBC local radio in the northeast of England.

He progressed from reporting on the non-league game to League football and eventually to the Premier League and worked for a number of local and national radio stations, newspapers and magazines.

After senior and editor roles on a number of publications he became editor of *Shoot* magazine in 2000 and got the chance to meet and interview some of his own football heroes. He has since edited and written a number of publications and books on both angling and football, including the best-selling *Shoot Annual*.

UK £9.99
US $14.99